Praise for ~~Legendary~~

As high achievers, we want to create work that matters for people who care. And that requires a head for business and a heart for relationships that are deep and meaningful. Ultimately, we'll be remembered not for the money we left, but for the life we lived. Tommy provides a roadmap for success in love and money—thus creating a legendary life.

—DAN MILLER
New York Times bestselling author of
48 Days to the Work You Love

Trust me when I say you will not be disappointed reading this book. There are many books that describe what Tommy Breedlove is trying to teach us, but Tommy's book goes the full distance by giving specific, actionable activities to make positive changes to your life. I laughed, cried, and dug deep into my heart and soul while reading his book and you will too!

—MIKE HIBBISON
Vice President, Merchandising Building
Materials at The Home Depot

We're all looking for ways to make positive improvements in our lives – both personally and professionally. *Legendary* is your map on that journey. This book takes you from personal stories to high-level thinking that will inspire you to be the best version of yourself. Invest your time here.

—CADE JOINER
Entrepreneur, Investor, Founder and
Board Chairman of Shred-X Corporation

Legendary is for the person ready to dive into entertaining, inspiring, and, ultimately, life-changing lessons and simple actions to better their lives. Author Tommy Breedlove's ability to tell stories masterfully combined with his willingness to share his personal journey will inspire you to dig deep and take action to make changes in your life. If you "do your job" by doing the simple steps outlined in this book, you can and will live the life you've always dreamed of!

—QUINCY JONES
Entrepreneur, Investor, and
Owner of SageStone Partners

Some books I read for pure enjoyment. Others I find myself sharing. Still others I study. *Legendary* is all of these and more. Tommy Breedlove has shared a book that should be mastered over a lifetime. Not only will the timeless words in his work improve your life, but, when applied, they will positively impact your entire world, just as Tommy has impacted and blessed my world.

—TOM SCHWAB
Founder & Chief Evangelist Officer,
Interview Valet

In his book, *Legendary*, Tommy teaches us how to become laser-focused on what really matters in our lives. He provides a blueprint for us to achieve significance, become fulfilled, and have fun without compromising our ambition or business success. Whether you are a driven, hard-working entrepreneur, or someone who thinks they are operating at a high level but missing something they can't put their finger on, this book will be nothing short of life-changing for you.

—MARC HODULICH
CEO and Cofounder of 29029

Most of us are living with our hair on fire trying to land the next big deal or make the next big move. Tommy is the authentic "real deal" who lives out the principles that he teaches in this amazing book. His practical and sustainable life practices will help us all grow into the Legends we were designed to be one moment, one day and one step at a time.

—TERESA MCCLOY
Business Coach and Creator of
the REALIFE Process®

If it's not a "Hell yes!" it's a "No." Remove the words "busy," "impossible," and "try" from your vocabulary. Find your zone of brilliance, say thank you, and avoid energy vampires. Those are just a few of the amazing takeaways from *Legendary*. It's a great book that made me look at my life in a much more positive way.

—DR. PETER BOULDEN
Entrepreneur, Dentist, and Founder
of Atlanta Dental Spa

I've been following Tommy Breedlove for years. Watching him speak, share his knowledge with others, and change lives is incredibly powerful. As a leader of a global IT organization who has long been seeking something more meaningful in my career and relationships, I can truly say *Legendary* is required reading for anyone who is ready to make simple, easy-to-follow changes for the better.

—TAYLOR BARNES
Vice President, CentricsIT

In *Legendary*, it's clear that Tommy spent a lot of time figuring out the qualities of those who've had the privilege of being called a "legend." To Tommy, it's not a matter of achievement, it's a matter of character. The inspiring stories and simple tactics contained in this book will help you truly live a life of success, fulfillment and significance.

—DEREK CHAMPAGNE
Best Selling Author of *Don't Buy a Duck*

We can choose to be as happy as we want to be. Often we get lost when life throws challenges our way. In Tommy Breedlove's book, *Legendary*, his wisdom makes us realize that we can live our best life by taking small, actionable steps to hold ourselves accountable for our happiness. This book is our success caddy. But our happiness is purely determined by our effort and commitment to be a Legend in our own life. And it's much closer than we think.

—BERT WEISS
Host of *The Bert Show*

In *Legendary*, Tommy discusses all the elements we need to become fulfilled and successful in our business and personal lives. Even better, he shares simple strategies anyone can use to improve in each of those key areas. To get the most out of Tommy's teachings, choose one area to focus on first and take action. Then move to the next. If you do, you'll quickly start building tremendous momentum toward living an extraordinary life.

—HANK MCLARTY
Founder and President, Gratus Capital

When you meet Tommy you immediately sense his powerful presence & gentle kindness. He has an effect on everyone that he meets. Tommy's story is inspirational and in *Legendary* he has distilled the essence of the way he lives his life. The lessons and exercises that he shares throughout the book will help any reader to live an intentional, fulfilling and "legendary" life.

—JOHN DOUGHNEY
Director, Global Client & Category, Auto, Facebook

Legendary

Legendary

Tommy Breedlove

...ORK

MELBOURNE • VANCOUVER

LONDON • NA...

Legendary

A simple playbook for building and living a legendary life, and being remembered as a legend

© 2020 Tommy Breedlove

Published in New York, New York, by Morgan James Publishing. Morgan James is a trademark of Morgan James, LLC. www.MorganJamesPublishing.com

ISBN 9781642795530 paperback
ISBN 9781642799538 case laminate
ISBN 9781642795547 eBook
Library of Congress Control Number: 2019941623

Cover Design by:
John Stapleton

Interior Design by:
Chris Treccani
www.3dogcreative.net

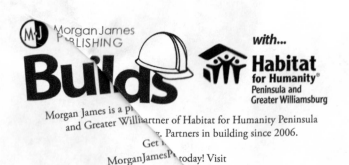

Morgan James is a pu... and Greater Willi...artner of Habitat for Humanity Peninsula and Greater Willi... ...z. Partners in building since 2006.
Get ...
MorganJamesP... today! Visit
...com/giving-back

Dedication

To my beautiful wife, Heather Breedlove. You are my rock and I am humbled and awed each and every day I get to spend with you. Thank you for always honoring and loving me unconditionally, even when I wasn't able to love or honor myself. Your grace, laughter, intelligence, and integrity are an inspiration to us all. Thank you for teaching me what love and being in love truly means. I am eternally grateful.

Table of Contents

Foreword xv

Preface xxi

Chapter 1 Take Action 1

Chapter 2 Living with Purpose 9

Chapter 3 Getting Focused 17

Chapter 4 Financial Freedom 27

Chapter 5 Conquering our Time 45

Chapter 6 Personal Mission Statement 55

Chapter 7 Our Inner Circle 61

Chapter 8 Blocking Out the Noise 73

Chapter 9 Mastering Our Mindset 85

Chapter 10 Living the Good Life 99

Chapter 11 Cultivating Unconditional Self-Love 109

Chapter 12 Intimate Relationships with Others 119

Chapter 13 The Power of Choice 135

Chapter 14 Never Giving Up 145

Conclusion 159

Recommended Book List 161

Acknowledgements 167

About the Author 175

Foreword

"Let me be clear."

Whenever I hear Tommy Breedlove address an audience with those four words (in his booming Southern accent), I get goosebumps, because I *know* whatever message he's about to deliver is going to change lives forever.

To backtrack for a moment: I first met Tommy at an executive retreat I helped organize near Atlanta.

The idea was for a group of 30- to 55-year-old professionals to take two days off from our lives for adventure, self-development, and yoga. As we planned the event, my fellow founders and I had no idea where to find a personal development expert we trusted—not just someone who had read a few books and collected inspirational quotes.

And then, somehow, we heard Tommy Breedlove on a podcast.

I immediately noticed there was something different about Tommy. He had a similar business background to the executives who would be at the retreat. He had climbed the corporate rungs to become a senior partner at a prestigious firm based in Atlanta—and realized he was a poor version of himself no matter how much money he made. Tommy quit his career at the top of his game. He made being the best person he could possibly be—a legend—his full-time job, and as a result of his hard work, he began serving others as a premier business and mindset coach.

Tommy soon became the *only* person we wanted to lead us through our self-development—and to our delight, he said yes.

At the beginning of the retreat, we were all sitting around the campfire, and I was asked to share my story, including how I had made it back from hitting rock bottom just a few months earlier. During my talk, I mentioned how much I loved coaching Millennial employees at 22squared, the advertising firm where I'm a partner. In doing so, I said, "I'm kind of like The Millennial Whisperer."

When my turn was over, I sat back down next to Tommy, who was staring at me with his scruffy beard and piercing blue eyes. A few moments passed before he kicked the side of my leg. "You better write that book," he whispered to me with such force that it felt like a command.

I took note but moved on and listened to each of the other executives introduce themselves and interact with Tommy. I'd never seen someone listen with such joy and concentration—it was as if the words each person spoke went straight into his soul. Tommy commented here and there but mostly listened with intent and in silence. (I don't believe he kicked anyone else . . .)

During the rest of the weekend, I experienced an incredible life transformation because of Tommy and watched him do the same for the others. High-powered executives were brought to tears as Tommy led us through guided meditations, purpose exercises, and authentic conversation. One guy decided to quit his job and travel the world for a year. Another, Bert Weiss, professed the newfound purpose Tommy helped him discover to his millions of radio listeners. Almost everyone at the original event is now doing more inspiring, impactful work.

I also experienced tremendous peace and growth throughout the retreat. Then, two weeks later, Tommy would be the catalyst for my biggest life transformation yet when he introduced me to his friend Nick Pavlidis. Nick's an expert in the book writing and publishing industry. Tommy was ensuring his comment ("command") to *write that book* was not just a nice little moment at the retreat but an action I absolutely needed to take.

Tommy was under no obligation to connect with me or any of the other attendees after the retreat was over. However, in very Tommy fashion, he was truly invested in each of us, individually, and in our success. Less than 18 months later, my book, *The Millennial Whisperer* was in bookstores everywhere and became a national bestseller. I've since built a very successful practice around the book. My mission now is to help leaders and their companies attract, retain, and lead Millennials impactfully and successfully while also making deeper connections with Millennial consumers.

I would never have done any of this without the love, support, and sometimes kick in the gut from Tommy.

I've since become best friends with Tommy and hired him numerous times to coach many of my friends and professional colleagues. Without exception, each of them has been completely transformed by Tommy's guidance, direction, and support. One colleague in particular went into his first coaching session very skeptical. He was *not* into self-development but agreed to participate in one session because he was feeling as if his life had hit a plateau. After the first meeting with Tommy, this extremely accomplished man called me and said: "That was the single most productive two hours of my life. And you know what makes Tommy different? He actually understands business and all things money, and drastically impacted my finances!"

Quite simply, Tommy's one of the greatest human beings I know. He's genuine and empathetic. He wants to change the world (and has already started doing so). I guarantee that Tommy will touch many lives with his influence and by opening up this playbook with us.

I saw Tommy struggle while developing *Legendary*. Like many of us, he still struggles with perfectionism, especially at his craft—and you'd better believe that what he has is a craft. It took nearly two and a half years of writing, rewriting, and editing this book multiple times for Tommy to finally say, "Chris, the book is good—very good—and was exactly what I needed when I was ready to make dramatic changes in my life to reveal the person I knew I could be." I knew right then this book was finally ready for the world.

People I know who have connected with Tommy have become better spouses, parents, employees, executives, leaders, and overall better people. Tommy knows what it means to build and live a Legendary life. He's helped hundreds, if not thousands, of other people begin their journey to becoming the best versions of themselves without sacrificing their hopes, dreams, ambitions, and financial success.

The world needs Tommy now more than ever before. Loneliness is an epidemic, and most of us ambitious, driven people are scared to ask for support and advice. We *must* commit to getting help. We *must* commit to self-care. We *cannot* allow ourselves to crumble on the inside because we feel stuck, unworthy, or even forced to live someone else's vision for our lives.

As you read this book, please know you are reading the words of a man who risked *everything* he had to discover what it means to live a Legendary life of hope, authenticity, and acceptance. Once he discovered the formula, he refused to return to the corporate world. Instead, he dedicated his newfound perspective and the rest of his life to helping people just like you and me to learn what he learned so each of us can become Legendary.

You might not be sitting next to Tommy staring at you and kicking you in the shin to take action. But please know he is there for you and wants the best for you. Take Tommy's advice: each day that you read, pick one small thing that resonates with you and start doing it. Over time, it *will* change your life in the same way Tommy has changed mine. And if you want help, reach out to Tommy directly, just like I did after hearing him on that podcast.

There's never been a better person or a better time for our Legendary journeys.

Let's do this—the best is yet to come!

—CHRIS TUFF
bestselling author of *The Millennial Whisperer*
and a partner at the Atlanta-based
22squared advertising agency.

door prison system. You're never coming back to this place again." At the time, he cared about me more than I cared about myself.

When I was released from jail, most of my friends and family disowned me. Again, rightfully so. I had nowhere to go except to work. So, I took a job at a plastic nuclear waste container factory. It was brutal. I was wrapped in thick protective clothing from head to toe in a warehouse baking at more than 100 degrees—on a cool day.

My job involved picking up eighty-pound plastic containers and then using a seventy-five-pound machine to cut off the tops. Over and over again, for eight hours a day, and for only $6 an hour. I smelled so bad from the plastics my roommate made me change clothes before entering our apartment after work.

Still, there was hope in the form of night college, but not easy at $6 an hour. There were times when my car broke down and I had to pawn the title to afford the repairs. It was a tough year and a half of my life, and I eventually had hernia and back surgeries due to the wear and tear on my body.

From a Cage to a Corner Office

One day my old man showed up at my apartment; I couldn't remember the last time I'd seen him. He looked around and said: "You have to get out of here. I've been following you. Your grades are excellent, and you're working your butt off—you deserve better. What do you think about applying to the University of Georgia?"

I replied, "What!? How are we going to afford it?" He might as well have said Harvard, Stanford, or Yale. My family had never attended college, much less a major university.

My dad replied, "I don't know, but we will. We'll finance it."

So, I ended up at the University of Georgia, where I plugged in academically and socially. I received amazing grades and joined every honors and business fraternity possible. No way was I going back to the factory or, more importantly, a jail cell.

As a result, a very large financial consulting firm, one of the largest in the world, actually, invited me for an interview and to stay at the Ritz-Carlton in downtown Atlanta.

The all-day interview went well, really well. I was overwhelmed when I received the offer, approximately $35,000 a year, which seemed like millions to me—more money than I could have imagined after my $6-an-hour gig.

I invited my best friend, Heather, to celebrate with me at Bones Steakhouse, which we absolutely could not afford at the time. (We were to become engaged at Bones just a few short years later and are still together this day. Not too shabby for a boy from the south side, huh?)

Thus began my foray into the professional world of financial consulting and public accounting: from a jail cell to working at Deloitte & Touche in just three short years.

Fast forward fourteen years. I was now a principal and leader of one of the largest financial firms in the southeastern U.S. I owned and wore suits for work—*tailored* suits. I'd made it. I'd achieved the American Dream, or so I thought. So why was I so freaking miserable and lost?

I couldn't shake the wounds and demons from my childhood. As a young boy, words and fists had been beaten into me, and I was taught I was unlovable, unworthy, and was never going to be good enough.

I had become a selfish, destructive, self-absorbed, arrogant bully as I chased money and power. After nearly a decade and a half of working insane hours, I had given up everything important to me. My marriage was teetering on the brink of divorce. If there was a checklist of 100 things *not* to do if you are a person of integrity, I had checked off 90 of them—YUCK!

For years, I had promised myself I just needed to close one more big deal or achieve one more corporate milestone, and everything would be better. I had promised Heather the same thing, and she stuck with me, no doubt hoping one time it would be true. However, it never happened. My happiness was always one bonus, one deal, or one meaningless milestone away.

True Freedom

This is when I found myself lying in an Atlanta ditch one ill-fated morning. There I was, looking up at the blue sky while weighed down with some very important questions.

After I picked myself up and somehow began to move on with my life, a marriage counselor suggested I attend an intensive seven-day workshop in Tennessee to help me discover why I felt and acted the way I did. Wow—it was and still is one of the best decisions of my life. This program cut me wide open mentally and emotionally for four days and then put me back together for the final three days. The counselors started me on a journey toward unconditional self-love, respect, and belief in myself.

Sound cheesy? Those were foreign phrases and emotions to me until I learned how to double down and truly invest in myself. In Tennessee, I finally saw I wasn't alone in my fears, thoughts, and insecurities. Many of my fellow attendees, from corporate CEOs and literal rock stars to normal, everyday people, were just like me—and chances are, a lot like you, too. We were all struggling in this human experience we call life.

I also met a new mentor, Kerry Geho, and I'll never forget the day I was in the middle of spilling my guts about my past when he said: "Stop talking! I have a question for you. Do you want to live your life, or do you want to continue to live your story?"

POW! His question hit me right between the eyes! I realized I had been letting my past anchor me down and dictate my present circumstances. It was a difficult but liberating realization. I'd never thought I had permission to be the man I knew I could be. At that moment, I decided to no longer live my past story and to start living my life. I would make my mental, emotional, and spiritual wellbeing my full-time job for as long as it took.

From that day on, everything in my life started to shift. As I began doing the hard work to better myself in all phases of my life, the most amazing things started happening. My network and friendships grew exponentially as new, positive, very successful people started appearing in my life. Even better, the negative people and influences who I allowed to drag me down into the darkness began to disappear.

It was beautiful. My professional life began to explode in epic ways as well. At work, I was elected to the board of directors and became a shareholder at 39 years old. My income doubled, and I went from being one of the most disliked partners in the firm to one of the most beloved leaders.

More importantly, I was living with integrity, self-confidence, and courage. For the first time in my life I was truly happy. I lacked stress, and my marriage was the best it had ever been. Heather even said to me, "This is the man and husband I always knew you were."

Then the most amazing turn of events started to unfold. Very successful ambitious people started asking me for help and guidance. They wanted to know how I had transformed so dramatically in just three short years. They wanted what I had. They longed to be happy. They craved purpose and meaning to their lives. They desired peace of mind and less stress. However, they demanded these wonderful feelings without compromising their business or financial success. They were and are my people—ambitious and driven—people who have a burning desire to be better!

After the 20th person asked me for guidance, I knew I could and would help thousands, if not millions, of other people, but I had to leave the financial world to do it. It was a scary thought as I was at the top of my game and set to make millions of dollars for the rest of my life.

However, I also knew if I didn't leave, I would be giving in to fear and letting my true calling in life swirl down the drain. I knew I would die with a massive regret if I did not take this giant leap of faith.

Eventually, and after a lot of great coaching and mentoring from my inner circle, I mustered up the courage, walked into a fellow board member's office, and told him, "I quit."

He just laughed and said, "Yeah, right." When he realized I was serious, he said (and I quote), "You're an idiot."

After a lot of back and forth, he added, "You know, Tommy, in the next few years, you'll be one of the highest earners in the firm." There it was. He was dangling the big-money carrot I had been chasing my whole life. I'm not going to lie. My legs buckled a little bit.

I took a deep breath, fully realizing I had spent my life running on a treadmill to nowhere. The power, money, and titles had not fulfilled me at all. I also 100% believed I could be tremendously more financially successful and personally fulfilled by doing something I loved and believed in. And you know what? I was 1,000% correct. So I said to him, "With all due respect, that is very humbling, but my soul is no longer for sale."

Building and Living a Legendary Life

I was free to become the master of my own destiny and follow my life's purpose.

I'm not at all suggesting we quit our jobs. We do, however, have to stop living our stories and start living our lives. We must do the hard work and invest in all phases (professional, mental, emotional, and physical) of our lives to become the humans we were born to be. This book will show you how.

After I left the corporate world and started coaching ambitious people on increasing their positive impact, the most extraordinary thing happened. I began seeing the formula for building and living a Legendary life.

Becoming Legendary is about finding the balance—between profitability and humanity, between confidence and vulnerability, and between working hard and having fun. Some legends are famous, but the vast majority are just like you and me—regular people who are relentless in the pursuit of their passions and leaving a lasting legacy for this world.

Now, as you'll discover in this book, Legendary status is within reach for all of us, and it will transform you, your relationships, your business, and your sense of fulfillment forever. Know this: I am no guru or sage on the stage. Nor am I a Legend as of yet, but I am damn sure working toward it! I will be walking this journey with you step by step, each and every day for the rest of my life. Now let's take this Legendary adventure together!

Carpe Diem!

Tommy

Chapter 1

Take Action

"It is not the critic who counts; not the man who points out how the strong man stumbles, or where the doer of deeds could have done them better. The credit belongs to the man who is actually in the arena, whose face is marred by dust and sweat and blood; who strives valiantly; who errs, who comes short again and again, because there is no effort without error and shortcoming; but who does actually strive to do the deeds; who knows great enthusiasms, the great devotions; who spends himself in a worthy cause; who at the best knows in the end the triumph of high achievement, and who at the worst, if he fails, at least fails while daring greatly, so that his place shall never be with those cold and timid souls who neither know victory nor defeat."
—Teddy Roosevelt

The first time I read this quote, I found myself asking whether I was the man in the arena or the armchair quarterback in the stands. I had just started the book *Daring Greatly* by Brené Brown. When I read those words, my soul knew immediately, I was more the critic than the man in the arena.

I no longer wanted to be the person who died with his dreams still inside him. I decided right then to work the rest of my life on picking up my sword and becoming the man in the arena. I knew it wouldn't be a smooth journey. I'd fall. I'd get hurt. I'd fail, and I'd have scars. However, I was committed to doing everything I could to building the best life for myself, my family, and the world around me.

This meant leaving my lucrative job in the financial world, so I gave my notice and began what has been a nearly decade-long journey of reflection and self-improvement, along the way committing to helping myself and others build and live Legendary lives.

If there's one thing I learned along the way, it's the power books can have in our lives. So, congratulations! You took action to buy this book and start reading it. You're in the arena. You have now begun the process of building and living a Legendary life.

Start Small and Dream Big

We all have big desires and dreams, especially as children. For most of us, those desires and dreams don't last until adulthood. We've been taught they're foolish or no longer attainable—both are 100% untrue. Building a Legendary life is possible if we take action—and *only* if we take action.

We will never achieve greatness or accomplish our dreams by only reading books. We must apply the information from those books to our lives. Without action, there will be no achievement. The secret to action, however, is to move forward by taking baby steps. Taking one small step at a time allows us to start from wherever we are and make consistent progress toward our dreams without becoming overwhelmed or frustrated.

"Action is the foundational key to all success."
—Pablo Picasso

It's also never, ever, ever too late to start. Whether you're 18 or 98 years old, you still have time to accomplish your goals and deepest desires. At age 45, Henry Ford created the revolutionary Model-T car. Stan Lee created the Fantastic Four on his 39th birthday. Julia Child was 50 when she started her career as a celebrity chef. The list of people who found success later in life is long. It's never too late to start if we keep going and refuse to give up.

There's also no shortcut or magic pill. Nobody achieves great things in life overnight. (In fact, the faster your ascent, the harder it is to sustain it. Just ask any lottery winner.) People who achieve sustained success put in years upon years of hard work in the arena.

Will you commit to taking action toward building a Legendary life with me?

Let's start small and dream big. Let's just commit to starting!

Everything we discuss in this book is designed to help us take sustained action—to help develop the hard and soft skills we need to achieve greatness and push through when times get tough or things are not working as fast as we want them to.

"We automatically land in the top 10% by simply showing up and honoring our commitments to ourselves and others. Taking *sustained* action will put us into the top 1%. Finishing what we start will put us into the top 0.1% in whatever we do."

We are Not Alone

Taking action toward building a better life can be scary and takes great courage. Most of us become consumed by fear when dreaming about a better future. We fear we will fail. We fear we will not have support. We fear people will laugh at us. Many of us even fear success. We fear we won't be able to sustain the success we achieve and will fail publicly when we inevitably collapse.

Fear is often our biggest obstacle and keeps us frozen where we are.

We must know that we are not alone. We're all afraid when we're uncertain or when starting something new. No one is immune to it. We can combat fear only when we accept it as inevitable. I've found these five truths about fear from the book *Feel the Fear and Do it Anyway* by Susan Jeffers very helpful.

1. The fear will never go away as I continue to grow.
2. The only way to get rid of the fear of doing something is to go out and do it.
3. The only way to feel better about myself is to go out and do it.
4. Not only am I going to experience fear whenever I'm on unfamiliar territory, but so is everyone else.
5. Pushing through fear is less frightening than living with fear.

Do any of these resonate? They sure do for me, but it feels amazing to know that we are not alone in our fears.

We'll talk more about fear throughout this book.

Important service announcement: we must accept the *only* cure for fear is action. We must feel the fear and do it anyway!

"Do or Do Not; There Is No Try."—Yoda

I once gave a small exercise to a client for shifting his mindset to achieve what he desired. He said he would try. The word *try* is code for "I will never do this as it is not important." (Ultimately, my client's lack of action cost him the results he wanted. Every time he "tried," he failed. He—like us all—only made progress when he stopped "trying" and started "doing.") Thank you, Yoda, for providing us with the profound quotation above.

When we say we will try, we aren't committing to the action and therefore never reach our goals. We need to eliminate this word from our vocabulary, one of the many "good for nothing" words throughout the book.

I start this book with taking action because if you're only going to "try" or are not ready to take even the smallest step, stop reading. Intention and desire without action is just hope, and hope is not a strategy. If you aren't ready for action, read no further. You're wasting your time (but thank you for buying my book). This book and I will be here when you're ready. Leave this book in sight, however, so it will be within reach when you're ready and willing to take action.

Nothing is Impossible

Nothing is impossible if we get started, keep going, and finish the drill. In fact, I keep this sign close by to remind myself and my team to take the word "impossible" out of our vocabulary.

Think about it: people are now working on taking humans to Mars and colonizing the Moon. Nothing's impossible!

Let's Climb this Mountain Together

Here's the beautiful thing about taking courageous action and doing the work outlined in this book. It's like climbing a mountain. As we continue to climb (or do more and more of the work), our view becomes better and better. View, in this case, is an analogy for success, happiness, peace of mind, and, ultimately, significance to life.

However, we must prepare for one problem. Most humans refuse to take action on improving their situation in life and therefore never begin climbing the mountain of all things self-improvement. Because of this, they're never able to see what we see and feel what we feel when we ascend on this journey of building and living a Legendary life.

I've been climbing this mountain since I turned 36 years old, and I promise to make the commitment to you and myself to never stop climbing until my very last breath. The view many years into this journey is absolutely spectacular. If you're ready to start climbing, know this for sure—I'll be right next to you along the journey.

Let's climb this mountain together.

LEGENDARY ACTIONS & REMINDERS

- List all of your dreams, from your childhood to now, regardless of how big or small.
- Pick your top three, and eventually narrow the list down to your number-one dream.
- Remember to dream big but start small. Take one small step each week to begin working toward this dream. (If you get stuck, please see the "Begin with the End in Mind" section in Chapter 3.)
- Remove the word "impossible" from your vocabulary. Ask your close friends and family to remind you of this whenever you say this filthy, nasty word.
- Remove the word "try" from your vocabulary. Remember, anytime we say we will try something, we are telling the other person it is not a priority and we will most likely never get to whatever it is. Ask your close friends and family to remind you of this whenever you say this horrible, no good word.
- Give yourself a moment of gratitude and love for having the courage to buy this book and taking action to build and live a Legendary life.
- If you do nothing else, remember this:
  - The only way to get rid of the fear of doing something is to go out and do it.
  - Not only am I going to experience fear whenever I'm in unfamiliar territory, but so is everyone else.

P.S. Also give yourself a big hug from me!

Chapter 2

Living with Purpose

My friend Lane Beene grew up in north Texas and (in his words) lived an ordinary life. He was an average student and a pretty good athlete—until he visited a nearby air force base and immediately *knew* he wanted to become a fighter pilot the moment he saw the fighter jets. From that point forward, Lane focused solely on this vision. He would need to excel in both athletics and academics, so he studied and trained hard. All the work paid off when he was accepted into the United States Air Force Academy, even becoming captain of the football team. He flew F-16 fighter jets for the U.S. Air Force for 27 years.

Lane's story exemplifies one vital truth about the importance of living with purpose in building a Legendary life. Before he visited the air force base, he felt average, but when he saw those fighter jets, he found a greater purpose in life and started to excel. Knowing his purpose pushed him to take the actions necessary to go from unremarkable to exceptional. Now retired from the U.S. Air Force as a Lieutenant Colonel (thank you for your service, my brother), Lane has found a new purpose in real estate development and investing.

The beauty of purpose is how it changes with us as our lives and passions evolve. Lane still loves flying, but his passions have shifted toward a new pursuit. He's now more fulfilled by helping people make money via real estate investing than by flying commercial jets, as many of his former peers do after leaving the military.

What is Purpose?

Simply put, our purpose is the reason we were put on this Earth. It represents who we are, where we are going, whom we want to serve, and the value we want to create for ourselves, others, and the world around us. It's where we find meaning, fulfillment, and significance in our lives.

Although our purpose evolves, as Lane proves, nobody can ever take it away from us. Only *we* get to decide what our purpose is.

Finally, as with many things, the more we learn about ourselves, the more we learn what our passions are. Thus, our purpose will evolve and change throughout our lives until our very last breath—which is what makes purpose so powerful and fulfilling.

The Importance of Finding Our Purpose

Discovering our purpose is important as it matches our actions with our passions (what we love doing). In sports, any professional athlete will tell you the game isn't won on game day, it's won during the practice and planning. Game-day execution is critical, but preparation determines 80% of the results.

What does this have to do with purpose? Everything. Finding our purpose helps us enjoy the day-to-day mundane tasks in pursuit of a higher calling. Lane spent *countless* high school hours studying and training with nobody around learning what he needed to do in order to be accepted by the Air Force Academy. He would never have done all the hard work if he hadn't been truly passionate about becoming a fighter pilot.

When we design our lives around our purpose, something magical happens. We look *forward* to doing all the hard work nobody else wants to do. We then get better and better and eventually become world-class—Legendary, even.

Discovering Our Purpose

I have a simple formula for finding our purpose during any season of our lives. First, our purpose is something we love. Lane loved flying jets and now loves real estate development and investing.

Second, our purpose is something we are talented at. Lane was good in school and athletics and worked hard to become exceptional at both. He then applied the same grit to become a world-class pilot and highly accomplished real estate professional.

Third, our purpose is something we believe the world needs. Lane is passionate about serving and protecting his country and believes the world needs freedom and democracy. He is also passionate about creating homes people love and feel safe in. Nobody can take these beliefs away from him.

When something checks all three boxes, we inevitably find greater fulfillment in our lives through serving others. Our careers are often unrelated to our purpose, which is A-okay. If our jobs are not directly related to our higher calling, we can use our talents and the wealth our careers create to advance our purpose elsewhere.

However, if we are able to match our profession to our purpose, fantastic. Our work will stop feeling like work altogether. And on occasion, time will literally stop, as we will love our craft and be completely fulfilled by it as well. How awesome is that?

Purpose Formula
We love it + We are talented at it + The world needs it

=

Our Purpose

If we want to match our career to our purpose, we use the following formula:

Matching Our Purpose to Our Profession
We love it + We are talented at it + The world needs it +
We get paid for doing it

=

Our Purpose via our Profession

Creating Our Purpose Statements

To aid in this process, our next step is to create our very own purpose statement. This keeps our purpose top of mind so we can make better choices regarding what we pursue personally and professionally.

For example, my current purpose statement is:

"Empowering humans to build and live Legendary lives. I will accomplish this via coaching, public speaking, and facilitating masterminds and retreats. As a result, my clients will experience greater professional and personal success, increased happiness, and lasting fulfillment and meaning to life."

Whew—that's a mouthful, but as you can see, my purpose statement checks all three boxes of the purpose formula:

- What I love (empowering humans)
- What I'm talented at (getting the most and best out of people through coaching, public speaking, and facilitating masterminds and retreats)
- What I believe the world needs (people need and seek more personal and professional success, happiness, fulfillment, and meaning to their lives).

I personally walk all of my clients through creating their purpose statement as this work is both an art and a science and requires deep listening. I believe finding our purpose is critical as I've experienced its life-changing results firsthand both for me and my clients. This is also an exercise we need to revisit throughout our lives regardless of our age or profession.

Some of my favorite clients are retirees looking to find a purpose for the next season of their lives. The excitement of golf, beach time, and travel wear off quickly in retirement and eventually fail to fill the void of feeling valid, valued, and a contributor to society. Many of my retired clients have come to me feeling a lack of fulfillment in service to themselves and others. Each time, I've known exactly what has been missing: purpose. When we have found their new purpose, their joy and fulfillment have both significantly improved. There's nothing wrong with fun, rest, and travel, but eventually we want and need more.

Writing Your Purpose Statement

Find a time where you know you won't be interrupted. Turn off your cell phone and computer, and grab several sheets of paper and a pen. (Yep—put pen to paper. You guys remember what those are, right?)

Write down "Things I Love Doing" at the top of one sheet of paper, "Things I'm Talented At" at the top of another, and "Things the World Needs" at the top of the third. On each sheet of paper, write down as many items as you can for each category. There are no wrong answers.

Write the first answers that pop into your head. Don't edit or overthink it. Be honest, though. Don't write "cooking" on the talents page if you've only microwaved popcorn. The more specific you are, the better.

Once you're done, take a few minutes to create a short, first-draft purpose statement inspired by what you wrote on the pages. Remember, this is a living, evolving statement. The goal is not to capture everything about who you are and what you want to do in one sentence. Getting a complete first-draft statement is always better than struggling to be perfect!

For a first-draft purpose statement, feel free to use the following formula:

My purpose is to [*things I love*] by [*things I'm talented at*] so I can help [*things the world needs*].

Use my purpose statement I shared above as a guide.

As long as your purpose statement reminds you of the things you love, the things you are talented at, and the things you believe the world needs, you've got it. Give yourself a big pat on the back from me for a job well done!

Moving Forward With Greater Purpose and Energy

When my clients and I complete their purpose statement, they immediately experience an uptick in excitement and motivation. By nature, my clients are ambitious and desire to be the best leaders and people they can be. They crave respect, love competition, enjoy winning, and strive to be as successful as possible. Finding their purpose gives them the final missing pieces of fulfillment and meaning in their lives.

"You don't need to change your job to be happy; you just need a change of heart."

LEGENDARY ACTIONS & REMINDERS

- Our purpose is the reason we were put on this Earth. It represents who we are, where we are going, who we want to help, and the value we want to create for ourselves, others, and the world around us. It's where we find our meaning, fulfillment, and significance in our lives.
- Continue to return to the purpose exercise during transitional phases in your life.
- Visit TommyBreedlove.com/Legendary to go deeper with discovering your purpose.
- If you do nothing else, create your purpose statement for this season of your life using the guidelines above.

Chapter 3

Getting Focused

Kevin Ouzts grew up in a home where food and cooking were a way of life. His dad regularly cooked using secret family recipes, while his mother prepared sides and desserts, to create uniquely delicious meals. Kevin's mother also managed a restaurant in the Atlanta area for fifteen years. It's no surprise that Kevin developed a sophisticated palate and passion for high-quality foods.

After graduating, however, Kevin began working for large corporations, which were a terrible fit. He knew deep down in his heart that he would find much more passion and possibility in the culinary world.

Kevin enrolled at Le Cordon Bleu and then took an eight-month unpaid internship in Napa Valley at one of the most prestigious restaurants in the country—The French Laundry. At night, he worked with a master charcutier, and instantly fell in love with the craft. "What is charcuterie?" you might ask. Great question: it's the business of preparing and assembling quality cured meat products.

Kevin found his culinary calling. It was a risky investment with borrowed money, but he and his wife, Megan, were all-in and dove headfirst into the charcuterie business. Ten years later, the Spotted Trotter has expanded into more than 48 states, and its products have been featured at the Masters Golf Tournament, Delta Airlines, and in prestigious restaurants and hotels all over the country. It is also featured in the Breedlove kitchen on a regular basis—we love having close chef friends!

Kevin and Megan's story is a great example of three important lessons of getting focused in order to build and live a Legendary life. First, we must define success for ourselves and ignore the opinions of others. Pursuing success in the culinary world was vastly different for Kevin compared to success as defined by his college classmates.

Second, we must set goals and use reverse engineering to achieve our definition of success. Kevin's relentless pursuit to learn best practices in the culinary world exemplifies the goal-setting and reverse-engineering process well. He studied at Le Cordon Bleu, took an unpaid internship, and started selling cured meats at farmers' markets. He dreamed big but started small with very specific, actionable steps.

Third, we must commit to living and working where our passions and talents intersect. I call this sweet spot our "zone of brilliance." Kevin enjoys and uses his God-given talents every day to provide exquisite balance in flavor, price, and sustainability with his food.

To summarize, the three pillars of getting focused are defining success for ourselves; setting goals and reverse engineering to the smallest actionable item; and working and living in our zone of brilliance.

Defining Success

Success for me is ensuring I experience and live life to the fullest without compromising my ambition or drive. A piece of this is being financially free and successful in business. I know when I'm successful in business, lives are being changed and impacted for the positive.

However, society and our media have taught us success comes from large houses, luxury cars, fancy clothing, and prestigious careers. Let me be clear: I absolutely love all of these wonderful things. I also learned the hard way they alone won't make us happy.

After all, if we own all the shiny toys in the world but don't get along with our spouse and children, or enjoy our career, would we consider our lives successful? Material things do not address our fundamental needs or desires as humans. In order for us to be truly fulfilled, we must prioritize our time, important relationships, and our needs for rest, exercise, safety, and, ultimately, peace of mind.

What if we decided to follow a different measure of success? What if success impacted our every need and included our deepest desires for our business and personal lives? Sounds wonderful, if you ask me!

Finally, included in my definition of success is continuous personal growth and learning, time with my closest friends, walking with my hounds, traveling, and a fun and loving relationship with my wife, Heather.

Instead of living a version of success forced upon us, let's live life on *our terms*. I recently found a powerful definition of success that goes right to the point of my core beliefs. It simply read, "Success—the accomplishment of an aim or purpose."

YES! I absolutely love this definition because it's the accomplishment of a purpose! Like most timeless pieces of wisdom, this is adaptable to anyone's unique dreams. When we match our deepest desires with our chief aim or purpose in life, we are successful no matter the outcome.

Begin with the End in Mind

What have you been considering starting? A business, exercise program, new career, or relationship? What is the overall vision for your dreams, and what does the end result look like? Write down your goals and dreams. No goal is too big or impossible!

"Remember, dream big and start small!"

Writing down our goals is the first action we take to turn our desires into reality. A Harvard Business School study shared the 3% of students who wrote down their goals before graduation were making ten times as much as the 97% who hadn't, ten years later.[1] WOW! Another study determined people are 42% more likely to achieve a goal if it's in writing.[2]

Heather and I write our goals for every important facet in our lives. We start with our pie-in-the-sky vision of how we want to live our personal lives, including everything from travel, experiences, and finance to learnings, personal growth, health, time, and more.

Working together helps us create better goals than we could ever create alone. If you're in a healthy long-term relationship, please consider working with your partner to set goals you're both inspired by. Finding a system for this can seem difficult at first, but Heather and I now enjoy building epic goals together. Since implementing this, we've seen 100-times improvements in all areas of our lives.

Once we write our big vision, we work backward by listing all the steps necessary to get from where we want to go back to where we are now. This is reverse engineering and helps us create small, actionable

---

1   Acton, Annabel. "How To Set Goals (And Why You Should Write Them Down)." Forbes. Forbes Magazine, November 3, 2017. https://www. forbes.com/sites/annabelacton/2017/11/03/how-to-set-goals-and-why-you-should-do-it/#64f35763162d.

2   "Study Focuses on Strategies for Achieving Goals, Resolutions." - Dominican University of California. Accessed November 1, 2019. https://www.dominican.edu/dominicannews/study-highlights-strategies-for-achieving-goals.

steps. We're turning our big-picture dreams into a tactical road map. The key is to reverse engineer until we find *very specific, small tasks* we can do today.

This is a good test for our list of actionable steps. If we are unable to take action right now, our steps need to be smaller and more specific. Remember, Rome wasn't built in a single day, so be patient and work your plan. If we start with the end in mind and keep moving through small steps, it's only a matter of time before we begin to achieve our life dreams.

Important—with our list of steps in hand, the only thing left to do is take action and execute (and adjust as our circumstances change). Actions are the only way we will move the ball forward and make progress. You've got this!

Nothing is impossible! People once looked at the moon, wanted to go there, and figured out how to do it.

"A goal needs to scare you a little and excite you *a lot!*"
—Joe Vitale

Celebrate the Progress

My team and I not only track the progress of our goals but also take the time to celebrate small and large wins along the way. At the end of each week, Heather and I receive an email from Lindsey Makitalo, our practice manager, highlighting all the team's accomplishments. Lindsey celebrates both our personal and professional achievements for the week. We celebrate everything from going on a date night and closing a big deal to having lunch with a trusted network partner.

This email is pure goodness and allows us to look back and celebrate our amazing achievements and milestones. This simple tactic allows us to be grateful for our progress along the way. Recognizing the small victories forces us to notice and celebrate our progress and not become impatient or even worse, give up on our larger goals.

Goals Must Be Fun

Having goals and desires that are fun cannot be overstated. *The New York Times* bestselling author and speaker Jon Acuff believes goals *must* be fun if we want to achieve them. Otherwise, why even pursue them in the first place?

Working in the Zone of Brilliance

During my financial career, I dreamed of being like my friend and charcuterie expert, Kevin Ouzts, who is truly happy in his career.

Then I realized we can choose to work in an area where our passions, interests, and God-given talents intersect. When we do this work, time literally seems to stop. This sweet spot is our "zone of brilliance." For me, time stops when I'm on stage or coaching my fellow humans to become the people they were born to be.

Some of us, however, begin working in a profession for other reasons and initially miss our calling. There is hope. We are not alone. Some of us are pressured to pursue a career other people deem important or realistic. Perhaps our parents or teachers pushed us to do something based on *their* definition of success, safety, or prestige.

The good news is it's never too late to start—never! If you do feel stuck or unfulfilled in your career, take a minute to write out your talents and passions and begin building and pursuing a profession you can be happy in. If Kevin and I can do it—so can you, my friends!

Concentrating *Only* in Our Zone of Brilliance

Concentrating on our zone of brilliance allows us to make massive progress in short amounts of time. All we have to do is commit to spending just one hour a day in our zone of brilliance working on our top priority. Watch how quickly we begin to accomplish our goals. This is because we focus on using our natural-born talents while also enjoying the work we perform. Does it really get any better than that?

Important: When I say concentrate, this means no social media, phone, meetings, or email during this critical time. As I began entering my zone of brilliance, I noticed immediate and exponential gains in my happiness, success, and efficiency. This is perhaps the most impactful productivity hack I've implemented in my life outside of "If it's not a 'Hell Yes,' it's a no!" More on that amazing wisdom later!

My friend and *The Millennial Whisperer* author Chris Tuff says if you spend 70% of your time on your passion and what you love and the rest on the other minutiae, you'll be so much happier. My goal each day is to spend 50 to 70% of my working time, or four to six hours, in my zone.

This is a major reason I outsource almost every task in business and life I'm not talented at or enjoy doing. Life is too short, and time is way too precious to not do what we love. What can you take off your plate? Admin work, scheduling, grocery shopping, answering emails, or yard work? Start small. Eventually work toward outsourcing everything possible. Outsourcing allows me to fully concentrate my time on the activities that bring the most success and joy to my life.

Many people find they're more productive during just one hour of focus in their zones than they are in a regular eight-hour day. Eventually, we enjoy this work so much, we move our zone of brilliance time up to four or more hours a day—BOOM! As a result, incredible achievements begin to happen more often, and our happiness grows exponentially to boot! We become world-class, true professionals, and among the most productive people in our fields just by doing what we love!

Working Outside Our Zone of Brilliance Hurts Everyone

The more time we spend in areas outside our zone of brilliance, the more frustrating our days become. We stop concentrating on our bigger purpose or calling, which is often the reason we pursued our career or business in the first place. What was once a dream job can become a nightmare. We lose our passion. We burn out. We coast—or worse.

As we progress in our careers or the companies we founded, we slowly spend more time on other activities and focus less and less on our talents and passions. Instead (and especially as entrepreneurs), we find ourselves spread across all areas of the business including sales, operations, finance, accounting, administration, or, in most cases, all of the above.

Designing our working life so the majority of our activities fall within our zone of brilliance is no easy task. Founders are often forced to pay large amounts of attention to business-building and operating activities.

Professional advancement also often comes with additional responsibilities, such as supervising others. This is especially difficult because ambitious high achievers and entrepreneurs are passionate about their trade and hate being associated with anything but perfection (we like to believe and feel like we're in control—more on this later).

When we stray from our zone of brilliance, we move into areas we're less competent in (and some where we have *no* competence). In the end, we hurt ourselves because we aren't doing what we enjoy. We take away the chance for others to work in *their* zone of brilliance when we do everything ourselves. We hurt our family and friends from being stressed, frustrated, and often overworked. Our clients are affected as well because the quality of work eventually suffers.

When we put together the right team of people, each working in their zone of brilliance, to produce the best possible results, *everyone* wins. We win because we get to work more in the areas we enjoy. Our team members win because they get to do the same. Our clients and customers win because they get better products or services performed by people all working in their areas of enjoyment and strengths. Investors and other stakeholders win due to the extraordinary results.

Even better is the positive impact we create within our businesses, families, and communities at large. By defining success for ourselves, setting goals and reverse engineering to the smallest actionable item, and working and living in our zone of brilliance, we can use our talents to serve ourselves and others in the best way possible.

LEGENDARY ACTIONS & REMINDERS

- Define what success means to you. Make a list of your life and business goals—be specific and remember there is nothing too big or small. List them *all!*
- Start with the end in mind by writing down your biggest goals and work backward until you find the smallest action you can take today. Do this each day by completing the next smallest action to move you closer to your dreams.
- Find your zone of brilliance. List all of your God-given talents as well as the things you love to do. Find a career or build a business that utilizes this brilliance! If you do this, you'll never look back!
- If you do nothing else, commit to spending one hour a day in your zone of brilliance (being a pro). Remember, no social media, phone, meetings, or email are allowed during this time.

When you get this number to four hours a day, wow—it will be my honor to salute you, Mr./Mrs. Legendary Master Pro.

Chapter 4

Financial Freedom

Money! Cash! Wealth! Yes, *money*: one of my favorites. I love it, desire it, and understand its importance. It's energy—a tool, a scorecard, a super-powerful magnifying glass of our characters, and a result of the value we provide. Remember that word: result.

Let me be clear. Money allows us to live the life of our dreams and increase the positive impact we have on others. However, as Anne Lamott writes in *Bird by Bird*: Money won't guarantee you much of anything, except a more expensive set of problems. Some of the loneliest, most miserable, neurotic people have a lot of money. Money is a magnifying glass. If you're a really loving person, it'll allow you to spread that wonderful love and if you're an angry a**hole, it magnifies that."

I just love that passage and Anne's book!

As a former accountant, financial consultant, and auditor; and having performed countless transactions to buy and sell companies, I understand the power of money. As someone who had to pay for car repairs by pawning the car's title, I also remember what it was like to be *without* money.

Coaching and teaching clients about abundant-money mindsets, cash flow, debt management, and building wealth is one of my favorite things to do—period. However, we must remember: money is a result of the value we provide in the marketplace; good strategies; and systems for building wealth, legacy, and freedom.

Fellow ladies and gentlemen of the legends-in-the-making tribe, I know we all love to play, compete, and win, so let's do just that in the world of all things money. Buckle up, open your hearts and minds to new learnings, and let's get started!

Money is a Mindset

Money is simply a tool, system, and transactional device. On its own, it has no power, and whether we think of it as good or bad is totally up to us. Now, get ready for the "woo woo," but trust me, I have been on both sides of the money mindset, and switching my heart from scarcity ("fear") to abundance ("love") has been life-changing from a financial wealth perspective. Here we go, my wonderful people—let's step up and step in!

In my heart of hearts, I know humans with money, wealth, and the resulting power believe they are 100% worthy and deserving of it. Because of this abundance mindset, their energy, thoughts, and beliefs around money are different from other people who don't believe they're worthy or good enough to be wealthy. This is why most lottery winners go broke soon after winning millions—they never developed their money muscles.

Our finances are as intimate as our relationships, sexuality, and health, which is why thinking about money can feel so intimidating and scary. It's our job to educate ourselves and reprogram our thinking for good financial health. If you don't believe there's enough money for everyone, or if you believe you'll never be wealthy, you won't.

If I took every dollar, peso, and yen in the world and divided it up equally between the billions of people on this planet, I guarantee within 100 years, the majority of the money would be back in the hands of 5% of the population—the people who've developed their money mindsets and have positive energy around wealth. (This sounds like hocus pocus, but it's true: everything on this planet is energy, especially money.)

I wish I could give each of you the knowledge and experience I gained during my 20 plus years of public accounting and financial consulting. However, this knowledge would mean absolutely nothing if we don't believe in our hearts and minds we will ever be wealthy.

What do we do to begin rewiring our hearts and brains to be on the abundance side of all things money? There are four steps:

1. Build a network of like-minded people who understand money and are working toward building wealth. Your network is your net worth.

2. Understand the basic principles of money outlined in this chapter, and take action on these strategies.

3. Read and educate yourself on all things money and wealth accumulation. I have included some great starter books herein.

4. Finally, and get ready for the woo-woo: use daily affirmations to rewire your money mindsets from fear to abundance.

Your Network is Your Net Worth

One of the easiest ways to begin creating wealth, abundance, and knowledge is to not only build our networks, but also build the right ones. Our network includes our professional peers, referral sources, friends, and colleagues with similar core values, ambitions, and goals. A solid group of people who give as much as they receive in business, knowledge, and life is priceless.

Again, the key to a great network is trust. To gain this trust, we must all give as much if not more than we receive from each other. Over time, as trust grows, we'll make it our mission to ensure each person within the network succeeds at both business and life.

If we want to attract money into our lives, we need to associate with people who have a burning desire to build wealth, earn more money, and engage in the pursuit of knowledge to achieve all of this. My network is by far the strongest asset in my balance sheet, and it's worth is incalculable to me. Because of this, I protect my network like Fort Knox protects its gold.

One of my favorite activities on Earth is connecting like-minded people who have the same values and desires so they may lift each other up in business and success. Not a day goes by when I'm not connecting two humans I believe can serve each other. Doing this for my network has come back to me 100 times in connections, knowledge, and money. Remember, if you want to become wealthy, hang out with wealthy people.

I absolutely will not, however, hang out with wealthy people if they're negative and judgmental. The people I choose to network with are wealthy, abundant, and kind people. This has also made my life happier as the people I associate with are happy and giving.

One of the biggest questions I get asked by people who are young, changing careers, or expanding their network (or all three) is *how* to network. Here's the simplest way and what has held steadfast in my life.

We must give, not take. This means bringing something of value to the person and avoiding the attitude of "Let me pick your brain," which just means, "How can I use you?"

Why do you think billionaires are so guarded? Everybody in the world has an angle, an idea, or a pitch and wants to get something from them. (I've often seen this happen firsthand.)

Value doesn't necessarily come in the form of a customer, business connection, or advanced knowledge. It can come as an act of service, a kind and genuine word or gesture, skill or task, or bit of wisdom serving the person on the other side.

Also, watch out for the "I am your biggest fan" stuff! Nobody likes a fanboy or fangirl, and quite frankly, it scares people.

We must also be bold. Reach out to potential connections in the form of a kind letter, nice video email (thank you for the ninja trick, Pete Vargas), or a kind word in passing. Be patient, genuine, and touch base periodically over time. And here's the kicker: expect nothing in return. One day, when you see this person in public or at an event (notice I said "when"), be bold and go introduce yourself. If you've been contacting them regularly, genuinely, and kindly over a period of time without wanting anything in return, they'll remember you.

Finally, when you meet with someone for the first time, always, and I mean *always*, ask the other person, regardless of where you see them on the "importance in life" scale, how *you* can help *them*. It's important to actually mean what you say and have the intention of helping them.

Now, buckle up and get ready for a little bit more woo-woo, because this has held true for me and my clients. The more I invest in myself, especially in my mental and emotional well-being with the exercises discussed in this book, the more I become the master of my mindset and have unconditional love and respect for myself. This allows me to be present, give, respect, and shower others with love when I meet them. My investment in myself has been the sole biggest reason for my network being as strong as it is today.

Seriously, what I thought was a strong network during my career in financial consulting pales in comparison to what my network is now. Back then, the people in my network cared only about money, power, and what others could do for them. In fact, when I left the big salary and prestigious career, a lot of them thought I was crazy. I went from the top of their call list to them never returning my calls. (Nope, not bitter at all.)

Now those same people, however, are beating down my door just to get a glimpse behind the curtain of my powerful network. It may sound clichéd, but like attracts like, and the more I get in a positive, abundant, and serving mindset, the stronger and more powerful my network becomes.

I promise I do not say this to brag but rather to give you hope that if a middle-class boy from the southside of Atlanta can have world-class athletes, entertainers, businessmen, and inspiring thought leaders reach out to him for advice, counsel, and support, anybody can do it. (As I write, I have a little tear in my eye for the blue-collar boy who became financially independent.) I believe in you and know you can do it as well.

One final ninja trick for now: Every time you have coffee, dinner, or a nice conversation on the phone with someone in your network or a new contact, offer to connect them with someone else. The connection needs to be with someone you believe is either like-minded, has the same ambitions, or can help the original person. If you do this, they'll eventually oblige you with the same kindness. You're welcome!

The key to all of the above is to be genuine, truly want to serve the other person, be altruistic, and expect nothing in return. Come to think of it, all the great spiritual texts say the same thing. Interesting how that ancient wisdom still holds true today.

A Quick Note on Networking Currency

Chris Tuff, the bestselling author of *The Millennial Whisperer*, is one of my best friends and a networking genius. Chris reminded me recently that every person has a currency—something of value we uniquely provide to others.

Currencies may include time, money, connections, influence, or talent and may be exchanged for equal value in both business and life. For some people, this currency is access to in-demand people, places, or things. For others, it might be a specific skill such as listening and making people feel valued and valuable.

No matter if we're wealthy or poor, or where we currently stand in our careers, each one of us has a valuable currency. Understanding what our currency is and the value we provide is critical in building relationships and networking.

Remember, the key is to give more of your currency than you receive. Do you know what your currency is? Here's a hint: What do people come to you for help with?

The Basics of Being a Financial Pro (Anybody Can Do It!)

A powerful step in rewiring our mindsets around money is to educate ourselves. Over time, with our change in mindset, our network, and with this knowledge, we will create systems and structures for building wealth.

It saddens me that most households in the U.S.—some estimate up to 70 or even 80%—live from paycheck to paycheck. Enough is enough, my Legendary friends! It's time for us to take our financials and future freedom back into our own hands. I 100% believe that if you make the choice to do the courageous work, practice patience, and do what I suggest in the next few pages, you will begin to be the captain of your financial ship!

Regardless of where we are today, whether we make $20,000 a year or $10,000,000, there is always time to pick up the tools to build our financial house into a fortress. The stress will melt away, and we'll begin to feel free again from financial mistakes that are anchoring us down from the past. It's time to seize the day!

Okay, for most of us, the next section might be a little bit of a snooze. Grab a coffee, do some pushups, stand up, and pay attention. These items are important and when implemented will change your lives for the better financially. Stay with me, people!

Create a Written Budget

A budget is the best place to start, as it determines where we are, and will help us get where we want to be. On a piece of paper or preferably a spreadsheet, list out all your monthly cash inflows (salary, revenues, income, interest—yay!) and cash outflows (expenses—boo!).

Be as detailed as possible by category, especially for your expenses. For example, your categories might include but are not limited to these: house/rent payment, car payment, insurance by category, credit cards, student loans, gas, groceries, utilities by category, cell phone, internet, cable, spending money (restaurants, movies, Netflix, golf, travel, etc.). I like to break out my spending money (or discretionary; more on this later) by category to figure out if and where I need to make cuts.

Total the inflows and outflows to see if you're in a positive monthly cash position or negative.

Living on Less in the Short-Term

Once we know our detailed budget picture, we can use any of the excess cash at the end of the month to begin paying off debt (or investing, if we have no debt). Debt reduction (and eventually investing) is the starting place of building wealth using the tactics outlined in this section. If your outflows exceed your inflows currently, do not panic. First, know you are not alone. You might experience some short-term pain for long-term happiness.

If you are "in the red," review your budget to see what discretionary items you might cut—can you quit Amazon Prime (which makes it *so* easy to buy things on a whim), turn off cable TV for a short period, or dine out only once a month? Once again, be as detailed as possible, and don't hesitate to bring out the big ax for giant cuts.

Worst-case scenario, you might have to take on a part-time job (or two) for a short amount of time or move to a cheaper place to right the ship. This is A-okay, because as legends in the making, we take action!

Just remember, you're doing this now so you can experience true joy and financial freedom later.

It's important, if possible, to keep a bit of our budget for fun things, no matter how small they are, such as buying an ice cream or renting a movie. Again, these can be small at first, but it's important to reward ourselves regularly for a job well done on cutting back.

We also need to live a little (*little* being the operative word here). Also, there are so many free things to do for fun including parks, city walks (or, even better, hikes in nature), seeing friends at their homes, visiting nearby family, going to church, libraries, and more. Remember, I have been so broke that I was "po'" which means I could not afford the additional "O" and "R" in the word "poor." I always left a little for fun and small rewards, however. If I could get out of debt, then anybody can.

Killing Credit Card Debt

Each time we use a credit card, we spend 10 to 20% more than we would with cash. Quite frankly, credit cards and other high-interest forms of debt are killing us financially and are the enemy—period! We will not build wealth or find financial freedom until we eliminate these nasty demons from our lives. This is important. It takes discipline and patience but will be oh-so-worth-it when the debt elephant is off our shoulders!

Here's how to kill credit card debt:

1. Make a list of all debts from the smallest dollar amount to the largest to get the overall picture.
2. Make the minimum payments on all credit cards with the exception of the smallest balance. Put any excess cash you found from your discretionary budget items to this balance, above your monthly minimum payment. For example, if you

find $5 to $500 extra every month, put it here, and watch debt disappear!

3. Once you've paid off one credit card debt, celebrate on a job well done, you've earned it. Woot, woot! Then, take the entire amount of the minimum payment from the paid-off credit card, plus the excess you were using each month, and add these amounts to the minimum payment of your next smallest credit card balance. See what we're doing here? It's basic, but we're taking our payments (including the excess) from the first paid-off credit card and adding it to the next.

4. Do this time and time again until you've paid off all credit card debt, and start using the hard-earned money to start building wealth—YES! YES! YES!

Save & Invest

This is absolutely one of my favorite topics, whether I'm coaching clients, brainstorming with my mastermind, or learning from my coaches and inner circle of trusted peers. I could write a book the size of *War and Peace* on saving and investing. Hmm, perhaps my next book? Well, in the interest of time and the fact my publisher already hates my word count, I will simply say this on saving and investing.

Saving

Depending on who you ask, the experts say that over time, we need to save between four and 12 months of our monthly expenditures (cash outflows) as an emergency fund. This will allow us to avoid having our lives affected dramatically when the economy drops, we lose our jobs, or some other major negative financial event occurs.

Important: Do not begin adding to your emergency fund until you have paid off all your high-interest debt as the interest on your credit cards and other debt way outweighs the security, benefits, and interest income of saving money. Forgive me if this sounds a bit complicated, but the math works. Contact me or a trusted financial advisor if you have further questions or need additional help.

Investing

I believe, depending on what our budget allows, we need to invest somewhere between 1% and 20% of our excess cash flows into various markets. Investing is where true wealth-building begins, and regardless of our salaries, anyone can begin in small or large amounts when we have paid off the high-interest credit card debt.

The markets I invest in include stocks, bonds, real estate, advanced stock options, start-up companies, and more. Variety in our investing is the key word. The experts call this diversification and risk management. Stew on those two terms for a minute—UGH! Simply put, if we put all our eggs in one basket, we're in big trouble when something trips us up. Therefore, be sure to invest in various opportunities. Also, pick investments you believe you would enjoy learning about and exploring. (For us, we love real estate and all things dirt!)

This is a very complex topic, but a fun one, if you open your mind to it. Don't let it scare you, and if *this* human can learn it, then you can as well. Like anything else worthwhile in life, investing requires education, mentoring, and help from pros. Again, I love teaching this and watching my clients build wealth and become free!

Important: there are no bad questions! If you don't understand something about an investment or financial term in general, keep asking your trusted advisors until you do understand—it's their freaking job to help. If you feel like they're talking over you, they are. If they won't help you or won't stop with all the "I am super smart and use important lingo," fire them and find someone who will help you understand. You've got this!

Be Charitable

When we study truly successful people, they all have one thing in common. They give both time and money. They support people through mentorship, giving their knowledge to certain charitable organizations and serving their communities.

The statement "greed is good" comes from a scarcity mentality. Anytime we think, "What's mine is mine, and what's yours needs to be mine," we're thinking there's a finite amount of money and time. This is another "us vs. them" mentality. We must believe there is more than enough money for everyone, because you know what? There is.

"Getting rich is about enriching your life at the expense of others. Being rich is about using what you've been given to enrich the lives of those you serve."
—David Salyers

What I have found is the more we give and serve, the more people want to serve us.

I 100% believe how giving more than we receive in both time and money (especially money) aides us in becoming wealthy. Since I've employed this as a core value, my success and happiness have increased exponentially. One of my Legendary principles is giving 51% more than I receive. Here are some of the tactics I use daily to ensure I'm on the positive side of giving:

- Tip a minimum of 20% to waitstaff. In addition, always round up. For example, if a 20% tip is $13, round up to $15.

- Give to your favorite charities and round up. When someone asks you to give to a charity you believe in, do it, and always round up. For example, if your heart tells you to donate $70 to a charity, make it $100. Watch the way this makes you feel over time.

- As I've mentioned, "May I pick your brain?" is one of the worst questions ever. However, I do enjoy giving my time to those seeking advice on money, relationships, and mindset—to a point (see more Legendary networking tips earlier in this chapter). Every other week, for two blocked hours, I give away my time to brain-pickers. By limiting my calls to 20 minutes or less, I can donate my time and avoid resenting people seeking free advice and guidance.

Who knows, when we give our time and money, we might just become the miracle someone was hoping for. Does it really get any better than that?

Never Stop Learning and Growing Financially

Investing in ourselves for life is key to success and happiness. By buying and reading this book, you have done just that. Step two will be to take action and implement the strategies and tactics herein. Again, thank you for the trust and walking this journey with me as I, like you now, continue to strive to build a Legendary life every day.

"Investing in yourself is the best investment you will ever make."
—Robin Sharma

To me, some of the best self-investments are continuous education and coaching. Within the past three years, I have spent a significance amount of money to further my education in real estate investing, public speaking, and for my personal coaches and masterminds. Once again, I promise I am not bragging, just emphasizing how important learning is to me, our family goals, and my clients for the best service possible. I also invest in all of these to continually "sharpen my pencil" to be the best human I can possibly be during my limited time on Earth.

You, my friends, do not have to make a massive investment if you're just beginning your journey. For just a small amount of money, and sometimes for free with a library, you can begin investing in your education and taking action with the great resources below discussing all things money, wealth, debt, and investing. All of these are easy and incredible reads, and some of the books, I have read multiple times. Remember: these books and their incredible knowledge are meaningless without action and application. You will begin building a life-changing, abundance money mindset, and wealth immediately if you actually implement their strategies and tactics.

P.S. I require all my clients to read and work through these books. Therefore, when you decide to work with me in the future, this will give you a head start on your fellow aspiring legends—BAM!

> *Think and Grow Rich* by Napoleon Hill: Quite possibly the greatest book ever written, in my humble opinion. It will reprogram your mindset in and around money forever as well as guide you on living a Legendary life.
>
> *Rich Dad, Poor Dad* by Robert Kiyosaki: Change your mindset from an employee to an investor with this epic book. I have literally read this book three times and now have it on my annual must-read list.

The Total Money Makeover by Dave Ramsey: I wish this book was required reading in high school. It's the best and most easily understandable book on all things money, debt, and living your life financially free. It hits all of the topics of navigating our lives in today's financially driven economy and world. Pay attention to the play-by-plays and "how" to become financially free.

Unshakeable by Tony Robbins: Read and work Dave Ramsey's book first and then add the knowledge in this great book to your financial arsenal second. In a very easy and understandable way, Tony gives us education and advice on taking control of our financial future and ultimately building wealth.

Profit First by Mike Michalowicz: It's the best book on paying yourself first (what an amazing concept!) and implementing the solid systems and processes in your business and personal life to ensure your financial success. Side note: Mike is a rock star public speaker to boot and overall amazing human. Can you tell I love his work?

What's Next if You've Learned Everything So Far

When I first began this chapter, I wanted to share with you fine people my 45 years of tips, strategies, hacks, and learnings for all things money. My editors flipped and, as usual, they were right. Then I realized, *Wow, this is super overwhelming, and we must learn arithmetic prior to learning advanced algebra.* However, I did want to share a couple of important items to consider for learning or implementation for the moderate to advanced financially minded folks.

Seek, at a minimum, a basic understanding of the following items to advance your knowledge:

- Inflation: Why we are losing money exponentially on our savings accounts and being killed by "death from a thousand cuts"?
- Compound Interest: It's the fastest way to build wealth; your money can literally work for you. Also, related to this topic, if you are on the wrong side of compounding interest, your money will literally dwindle away to nothing—at the speed of light!
- Time Value of Money: Money today is worth more than money one year and especially five years from now.
- The Principles of Accounting: If you are an entrepreneur, this is a must as all businesses are built on the language of accounting; you'll save much time and heartache by investing in this small bit of knowledge.

These topics are outside the scope of this book, but acquiring this knowledge will allow us to protect ourselves against financial sharks and really take control of our financial futures!

Financial Affirmations

Truth moment: Due to my prior career, a zone of brilliance for me is teaching money and building wealth. However, even though I am an expert in all things money, I continue to write and say the following affirmations aloud daily. It might sound super woo-woo, but I promise you they have 100% worked for me and countless clients. The more we write and speak the affirmations aloud, the more we believe them and, eventually, they become a way of life for us. The affirmations to include in your daily routines are as follows:

- Success, money, and wealth make me happy and are very good for me and everyone around me.
- I am so grateful and happy that money, wealth, happiness, joy, and goodness flow easily, frequently, and abundantly to me.

In conclusion, my fellow beautiful Legends in the making, repeat after me: I am worthy enough and will have as much money and wealth as my heart desires. If you believe it, you will receive it!

LEGENDARY ACTIONS & REMINDERS

- Financial freedom, wealth, and money all begin with an abundant mindset.
- By using the steps in this chapter, begin creating a powerful network today. Remember, your network is your net worth.
- Read, understand, and take action on the following books. You'll begin building an abundance-money mindset and wealth immediately if you actually implement their strategies and tactics.
  - *Think and Grow Rich* by Napoleon Hill
  - *Rich Dad, Poor Dad* by Robert Kiyosaki
  - *The Total Money Makeover* by Dave Ramsey
  - *Profit First* by Mike Michalowicz
  - *Unshakeable* by Tony Robbins
- Write and say aloud the following affirmations daily.
  - I am so grateful and happy that money, wealth, happiness, joy, and goodness flow easily, frequently, and abundantly to me.
  - Success, money, and wealth make me happy and are very good for me and everyone around me.
- Find out what your networking currency is. Here's a hint: What do people come to you for help with?
- If you do nothing else, begin building your financial empire today by starting small and thinking big. Begin by:
  - Creating a budget
  - Living on less
  - Conquering debt
  - Saving and investing
  - Being charitable

Chapter 5

Conquering our Time

My father-in-law, Mike Hegwood, and I had a rocky relationship. Our issues were not on him; they were on me. This was more than 20 years ago, and up until I met Mike, I hadn't had many positive male role models in my life. I know he wanted to embrace me as family and to see if I was a good fit for his daughter. He wanted to ensure I would make her happy.

Eventually, Mike said yes when I asked for his daughter's hand in marriage and, over time, he became one of my best friends. More importantly, he became a much-needed father figure and positive role model for me to follow. He was strong as a horse, a good community member who owned his own business, and a great husband. He was all the things I aspired to be.

Both Mike and I wanted a loving relationship. We were just starting to get there, and an upcoming golf weekend was going to be an epic start to a lifelong friendship.

Ultimately, it was too late.

While eating dinner the Thursday evening before our trip, Mike started slurring and fell over. He was immediately rushed to the hospital.

When the diagnosis came back, we found out that Mike had stage four melanoma with three tumors in his brain and another four in his lungs; they were inoperable. The diagnosis was terminal and devastating. Our families watched Mike disintegrate slowly during the next three months. Mike was only 52 years old when he passed away. I was never able to experience what our relationship could have become. Heather and I had only been married for six months.

Looking back, I'm so grateful I was able to spend those six years with Mike in the good times and bad. I just didn't know how grateful I was for him until after he passed away. I had failed to find the time to truly nurture Mike's friendship, mentorship, and love. The clock had run out.

Given the time to grieve, I've also learned how my relationship with Mike reveals the importance of focusing our time on what matters most.

The goal of this chapter is to do just that. It will guide us through reconquering our time to concentrate on what matters most. Let me be clear. *Everyone* on Earth has the same amount of time on any given day —24 hours. So let's lean into all things time management and good habits to help us build and live Legendary lives!

"Time is a choice, and I have as much as anyone on Earth."

Prioritizing Our Time

In *The Big Leap*, Gay Hendricks writes, when we take ownership of our time, we get twice as much done—in half the time. When we say we're too busy or don't have time, we're lying to ourselves and everyone else. We *all* have the same amount of time in a day. The difference is, successful people choose to prioritize important people and tasks over everything else.

I've eliminated the word "busy" from my vocabulary. It's another one of those dirty, filthy, nasty words, like "impossible" and "try." Busy is code for being unproductive and something or someone else is controlling our time. Ultimately, we control our own time by the choices we make.

Another key to prioritizing time is to avoid striving for a perfectly balanced life. It's overwhelming to chase the elusive Loch Ness monster called "balance" especially because financial and life success will look different for every person. Even though balance is currently a sexy buzzword, most success-driven people, myself included, don't prescribe to a "work-life balance." We ensure we *prioritize and reprioritize* our time depending on our personal and professional goals.

If my marriage or wife needs more attention, I make her a priority over everything else. The same has held true for building a world-class public speaking and coaching practice.

If we want to build a successful start-up, we will need to spend the majority of our waking hours on our venture at the expense of time with loved ones and for fun. The key is to balance and rebalance depending on what we and our families deem most important to our success and happiness.

Over the years, I've witnessed many of my clients failing to prioritize and reprioritize until it's too late. They tell me, "When I get to this particular goal, *then* I'll focus on my health, family, or spouse." Let's be honest, *when* is like *more*. We never actually get there. We pile up incredible business success, houses, and nice clothes—and often have no one to share them with because we put everyone else last.

> "The rich invest in time, the poor invest in money."
> —Warren Buffett

We must fiercely protect our time by focusing only on the most important people and activities and saying no to everything and everyone else.

Time Blocking

One of the most powerful tools I've learned and implemented, especially with my practice, is time blocking. This is marking off time on our calendar, from one to four hours, to focus on the one, most important thing. My one thing was this book. When we pick our top priority, we must refuse to compromise the time we dedicate to the task—no phone, no email, no social media.

> "If you don't prioritize your time, someone else will."
> —Greg McKeown

I don't start my typical workday before 9 A.M. The early morning hours are my sacred time for my morning routine. This time is critical for me to nourish and invest in myself so I can best serve others. I rarely compromise this time, and when I do, it affects my whole day negatively. Because of the work I do, especially in coaching, I have to be totally in tune, fully present, and full of energy. My time from 6 A.M. to 9 A.M. each morning prepares me to give my 100%.

I also don't compromise my evening time because this is the time for Heather, fun, friends, and me. If I don't honor this time, what am I doing the rest of it for? Because I work in the pain and purpose business, I receive calls and texts seemingly 24 hours a day, but unless it is a true emergency, I don't respond at night.

Of course there are exceptions to all rules and boundaries, but if I am honoring these commitments 80% of the time, I believe I'm winning at this game we call life. For example, I *chose* recently to compromise my morning time because a client flew in from England and needed to meet early in the morning. Because he showed such dedication and commitment to me coaching him, I wanted to honor him and do the same. This was an extraordinary circumstance, however. And—wait for it—it was a definitive "Hell Yes!" (More on this in the next section.)

Part of time blocking is sharing our priorities and boundaries with our colleagues, staff, family, and friends so they know and understand when and why we are not available for them. (My teammates Lindsey and Patti are modern-day dictators when it comes to my calendar and protecting my time—they are the *best!*)

To help get us started on time blocking, we can start with just one hour a day completely to ourselves or for our most important work. Eventually our time block can increase to four hours a day of focusing on our zone of brilliance. When we implement this simple boundary, we will watch as our productivity exponentially increases. We will also begin teaching others, especially our family and teams, to properly take control of their time. Once they begin, they'll also see how time blocking results in significant increases in efficiency and overall financial success.

If It's Not a "Hell Yes!" - It's a "No."

This expression is the most powerful tool I have for truly owning *my* schedule. It is one of the biggest weapons in my soon-to-be-Legendary arsenal and one of the most life-changing strategies I've implemented in my day-to-day life. I don't know who came up with it, but it's genius. Walking my dog, Hodges? Hell Yes! Getting yanked into another dinner with gossiping and judgmental friends or colleagues? Nooooooooo!

As ambitious, successful human beings, learning to say no more often than we say yes (or Hell Yes!) is one of the easiest ways to conquer our time. I totally agree with a philosophy Gary Keller outlines in *The One Thing*: a single no is worth one thousand yeses.

As I've mentioned, the people we aspire to become don't have more time in the day than we do. They know how—and when—to say no. Our idols know how to stay focused and block their time through this one word. "No." The word *no* is also a complete sentence. They refuse to take on extra meetings, activities, and requests not because they're mean, but because they're concentrated on their passion—their Hell Yes!

When we are asked to do something—attend an event, have dinner with a friend, visit family on the weekend, etc., our guts know immediately whether it's a Hell Yes, normal yes, or a no. It's a visceral reaction. If it's a maybe, it's a no. It has to be an absolute "wow" yes to do it.

This takes practice, and to this date, I've only been able to do it 80% of the time. It's super hard to implement this with family and certain friends as our shame monster kicks in telling us we should go visit them even though it's like pulling teeth.

On a related note, the more we implement our Hell Yes strategy, the more we overcome the shame and fear around the things we think we "should" do. For example, if we don't want to go somewhere, let's not go. Regardless of what "they" say. Who are "they" anyway? (Much, much more on this in Chapter 8.)

I've eliminated the word *should* from my vocabulary. It's the single most shaming word in the English dictionary. Think about the last time someone said "should" to us. They were basically stating they know what's best for us more than we know what's best for us. Think of all the bad preachers, teachers, and parents in the universe. Should is another one of those dirty, filthy, nasty words, like *impossible, try,* and *busy.*

Ultimately, my fellow beautiful humans, this is our one precious life to live, so let's waste as little of our time as possible. Time, outside of love and health, is our most valuable asset. Ultimately, implementing "If it's not a Hell Yes, it's a No!" will lead us to be more successful in all phases of our business and personal lives—I promise!

Changing Habits

Conquering our time also demands good habits—and that doesn't just mean flossing your teeth twice a day. (Ugh—I am so still working on this. Flossing is one of my least favorite things to do—ask my dentist!) Like it or not, we have to kill our bad habits and create new positive ones to become Legendary. The difference between a pro and an amateur is habits.

Because habits become automatic actions, they free up our time to focus on our passions and purpose. Bad habits, however, can suck up our time and even shorten our lives if we are not careful—I don't know anyone who's become Legendary by binge-watching Netflix two days a week or cracking open that fourth beer at the end of the night.

Studies say it takes 21 days to form a new habit. To my knowledge, many yogis say 40, and one scientist has even said 60. I don't know which, if any, are true, but we have to practice habits *every day* for results to happen.

James Clear, the author of *Atomic Habits*, suggests the following simple rule, which I have fallen in love with. For any good habit you're implementing, don't miss two days in a row. Yes, so easy but also oh so hard! Sure, we can take a day off, but we need to jump right back on the wagon to truly make positive changes to our lives.

Remember, all of the items in this book are meant to rewire our brains and hearts to reveal the person we were born to be, so creating positive habits is one of the easiest and best ways to ensure we stay on the path to being remembered as Legends.

I highly recommend reading not only *Atomic Habits* but also *The Power of Habit* by Charles Duhigg. These fine gentlemen take a deep dive into killing bad habits as well as reveal how to develop and maintain healthy ones. For now, let's discuss their tactics on building a new, positive habit by identifying the cue, routine, and reward. Charles and James outline the four following clear steps to change any habit. I've also added a fifth tactic of my own that has worked wonders for me:

1. Identify the cue. As an example, Lindsey wanted to break her dessert habit at the end of dinner in order to cut back on sugar. The cue was the end of her meal.
2. Identify the routine. For Lindsey, it was reaching for something sweet right after dinner.

3. Experiment with different rewards. Instead of ordering cake at a restaurant or dipping into a pint of Ben & Jerry's at home (my personal weakness, ugh—d*mn you, Americone Dream), Lindsey first tried chewing gum and then practicing a few minutes of yoga. The gum, however, was short-lived and she wanted something she could savor. Doing yoga after a meal was great, but it was already part of her regular practice. Therefore, this experiment did not work and was not enjoyable, so she kept experimenting with other tactics.

4. Have a plan. Finally, Lindsey discovered that a hot cup of herbal tea fixed her craving for a treat.

5. Find an accountability partner. This is the fifth step I've added. I struggle with a consistent exercise routine, so I've identified a few people to help keep me on track. I report in to my friends Chris and Julie Tuff almost every day, and also work out with Julie at least once a week when I'm not traveling. My wife, Heather, is also my accountability partner—we follow each other's good or bad habits. If she's eating takeout Chinese or watching Netflix, I cocoon with her. When I see her cranking out 45 minutes on the Peloton and I'm considering watching another episode of *The Office*, I'll probably think twice and go out for a run instead.

By conquering our time, we'll surprise ourselves, and the world, with our newfound focus on our purpose and passion. It may not happen overnight and may be very challenging, but we can take small steps that result in massive benefits in our lives.

Eliminating the word *busy* and implementing time blocking ensures we spend one to four hours on the one thing that excites us most. We can eliminate the "shoulds" by implementing "If it's not a Hell Yes, it's a No." We can silence our phones, learn to say no, change bad habits to good, and we'll find not only more time but also much more success, fulfillment, and happiness.

LEGENDARY ACTIONS & REMINDERS

- "The rich invest in time, the poor invest in money." – Warren Buffett

- Eliminate the nasty, filthy, dirty words *busy* and *should* from our vocabulary.

- Forget about a one-size-fits-all idea of balance, and create your own schedule. Fiercely protect that schedule by time blocking and enlisting help.

- What's the one task you need to focus on for one to four hours a day that, by doing so, will move you closer to your primary goal? Time block one to four hours per day to dedicate to this pursuit.

- When we spend time being a pro on our "one thing," we see exponential returns quickly.

- Never miss a habit twice. Once is okay. Remember: whoever conquers the boredom and mundaneness of adopting new, good habits will be the most successful in life and business.

- If you do nothing else, practice saying no to things that are not "Hell Yes!"

Chapter 6

Personal Mission Statement

In Chapter 2, we created our *Purpose Statement.* Our purpose brings us fulfillment, meaning, and significance to this particular season in life. Our purpose can and will change over our lifetimes depending on our desires, goals, and dreams.

In contrast, our *Personal Mission Statement,* which is based on our core values, what we stand for, and who we'd fight for, typically does not change as it represents our deepest principles and non-negotiables.

When we base our lives on status, our money, and what other people think, we build very shaky foundations. The world can take all of these things from us in an instant as none of these are truly in our control. Therefore, we must build solid foundations for ourselves based on purpose, our core values, and a powerful mindset because it's not *if* life's suffering and tragedies will happen, it's *when.*

Creating a Personal Mission Statement is a re-centering and a crucially important step to building and living a Legendary life. Money, power, and success will always be important to us ambitious humans, and we can set goals accordingly. However, we're shifting our focus to our core values, so when the challenges come, we will be better equipped and ready to deal with them on a much stronger foundation. Over time, as we will see, the aim is for our mental and emotional fortresses to become impenetrable as we continue to do the hard work outlined in this book.

Setbacks will still affect us, but not nearly as much as they would without implementing the strategies outlined herein. We are solidifying who we are, where we are going, and who's coming with us!

We are doing the hard work moving us toward being a principled, purpose- and values-centered person (inwardly focused), as opposed to a person focused on money, career, or status (outwardly focused). We can always aspire to achieve these important external validations—I know I always will—but we cannot stand on or be defined by them due to their fleeting nature.

When we know our Personal Mission Statement and stand on a solid foundation of our core values and integrity, and then we experience loss, we don't break down. On the other hand, if we stand on our material things or status, when those things are taken away, we collapse.

Our North Star

No one will ever remember, care, or read our résumé at our funerals. What would our obituary say if we died right at this very moment? What would we *want* it to say? To discover who we want to be remembered for and what our core values truly are, we need to write our own obituary. What do we want to be known for, and what do we want those important to us to say about us when our life is over?

We can use our obituary as a benchmark and the beginning of our Personal Mission Statements. Now here's the most important part for us, after we come up with our statements: we must have a trusted group of peers to hold us accountable to these values. (More on this in the next chapter.)

Our Personal Mission Statement is our North Star, our Highest Truths as human beings. Our Personal Mission Statements reflect our souls, who we are, and what we aspire to be. We can always look for our North Star when we become lost, afraid, or confused with the direction of our lives.

We discuss looking in the mirror frequently in this book, and now is one of those times. Are we currently living these values? Would people stand up at our funeral and say what we have written? Or, are we all about business, making money, or obtaining power and fame? All of these are important goals for us and are all part of my personal goals. However, not one person will care about any of them at our funeral, and we all know the famous saying: we can't take it with us. People will remember how we made them feel, not what we achieved or possessed.

We can review our Personal Mission Statements at the beginning and the end of each day and ask ourselves, "Is this how I'm living my life?" If so, congrats to us; our lives will be filled with love, happiness, and success. If not, that's okay, because it's never too late to start again. We must vow to be better than we were yesterday, pick ourselves up, and strive to live the values starting right now and going forward.

One of the pillars to building and living a Legendary life is to stand on our principles. When we do, we prevent life's ebbs and flows from holding us back or bringing us down for any significant length of time.

Creating a Personal Mission Statement

A personal mission statement is based on our core values, beliefs, and what we want to hold ourselves accountable to as a way of living our lives. It's what we stand for and what we aspire to live by and stays pretty steady throughout our lifetimes.

Let's start creating our personal mission statements by writing down the following:

What are your non-negotiables in life? List 10 of them.

Now, write down the answers to the following questions:

What do you stand for? Another way to think about this is to ask what really angers you. Typically, when we see something in life that really upsets us, it is due to someone or something violating one of our core values.

What would you fight for, and why?

What are the "shoulds" following you throughout your life? I freaking hate the word "should," but it is so powerful here. The shoulds following us are actually our shame monsters for all of our unmet dreams—our regrets for giving up or not following our hearts and desires.

What are the life commitments you want to make to yourself, those you love, and the communities you want to serve?

Once you've answered the above, you are ready to create your statement. To help, here's a look at my Personal Mission Statement—the Legendary human I aspire to be remembered as:

I, Tommy Breedlove, hold myself accountable to the following core values that I hold so dear.

I will live with courage, unconditional self-love, and integrity, and constantly strive to make a positive impact on the lives of my fellow humans. I will be compassionate, empathetic, and kind. I will work every day to minimize my fears and insecurities and live life without judgment and anger toward my fellow human beings. I will live by the Golden Rule of doing unto others as I would have them do unto me.

I will love and respect the most important person in my life unconditionally—my wife, Heather. My actions will show that I love and support her, and I promise to be the same person publicly that I am behind closed doors.

My work and purpose are to give people the tools to build and live Legendary lives for themselves, their families, and those they serve. I will lead by example and not just talk the talk but walk the walk by devoting my time, talents, and money to this mission.

I will never stop growing and learning and will always be open-minded to the opinions and thoughts of others. I will continuously strive to better myself emotionally, mentally, physically, and spiritually. I will choose goodness in all of my decisions.

I will nurture and maintain 15 close friendships, prioritizing the time I spend with these important people. I will be present and listen deeply when spending time with the humans that I love and serve.

I will travel often. I will make time for fun, play, rest, and sleep.

I will remember that my time on this Earth is short and always strive to be better than I was yesterday.

I will serve others. I will live with a grateful, abundant heart. I will pray for guidance every day and honor God by honoring these core values.

LEGENDARY ACTIONS & REMINDERS

- Our personal mission statement is based on our core values, what we stand for, and what and who we'd fight for.
- Write your obituary. What would you want others to say about you when you are gone? Be as specific as possible as you might also see some of your unfulfilled dreams in this powerful statement of your life.
- What are your non-negotiables in life? List 10 of them.
- For 60 days, read your Personal Mission Statement first thing in the morning and right before going to bed. This will allow for memorization and for it to trickle down and embed itself into your soul.
- Important: Have a trusted group, an inner circle, to hold you accountable to your Personal Mission Statement and for all of your major choices going forward. (See the next chapter for details regarding our inner circles.)
- If you do nothing else, based on what you've written in your non-negotiables and your obituary, create your own Personal Mission Statement.

Chapter 7

Our Inner Circle

What if we could handpick the best people to guide us through our Legendary journeys?

Think about it. Books (especially this one) are powerful weapons in our Legendary arsenals as we step up and step in to being better than we were yesterday. Coaches are powerful resources as well. Imagine, however, if there was *always* a small group of trusted people available when we needed them. Wonderful humans who truly wanted the best for us in all phases of our lives. And even better, they make it their mission to keep us on the right track, mentor us, and give a kind word of advice or a swift kick in the rear when we need it.

Without exception, every Legendary human I've studied surrounded themselves with a team of trusted people. From Alexander Hamilton and Socrates to Eleanor Roosevelt and Bill Gates, influential people have all been influenced by someone else. A prime example is the modern-day Presidential Cabinet structure, which dates back to when American leaders John Adams, Thomas Jefferson, and others met regularly to support each other during the early days of the U.S.

Companies have boards of directors—trustworthy, experienced business people who guide the organization and help them build strategy and make important decisions. Athletes, entertainers, and artists have coaches and masters helping them consistently improve their game, manage their money, and improve their craft. Great entrepreneurs and leaders hire executive coaches and surround themselves with trusted colleagues and friends to help them make better choices in their businesses.

We, too, can have a personal board of directors, or what I like to call an inner circle. These are trusted coaches, colleagues, friends, and peers who help us take action and aren't afraid to share their opinion on our successes and failures. They're the people who push us in the right direction and hold our feet to the fire when we stray from our purpose and core values.

> "You are the average of the five people
> you spend the most time with."
> —Jim Rohn

To one day become Legendary, each of us must find our own team of trusted people to keep us accountable for achieving our goals, living within our value system, and continuously improving as humans. We create our own inner circle.

As someone who has long depended on my "board" to advise me on decisions, console me on failures, and celebrate my successes, I'm excited to share my tactics. These include carefully choosing—and reevaluating—

our inner circle members, along with setting appropriate boundaries and applying the "hire slow, fire fast" philosophy to our own lives.

Choosing the Members of An Inner Circle

Humans have always had inner circles. It was just simpler when we were tribal and indigenous. Regardless of race or continent, our elders were our trusted team of advisors for centuries. We celebrated the wisdom of those who came before us. Their purpose was to lead and bestow their wisdom and value systems on the younger generation—and ensure the younger people's drive to succeed didn't come at the expense of everything else.

Today, those ties with our elders are frayed, which means it's up to us to choose the members of our inner circle. Maybe it's five people, as Jim Rohn says. Maybe it's a little bit less or more. I, personally, have a group of 15 amazing women and men as a part of my formal inner circle, and I share some of their stories and much of their wisdom throughout this book. These are people I unconditionally trust, value, and appreciate.

When choosing our inner circle members, we must be selective and ensure each person loves and respects us. They don't have an alternative agenda or ulterior motives, they truly care about helping us achieve our goals, and they won't just tell us what we want to hear. They must be like-minded in their views and core values, and they must be *abundance-based* thinkers, not fear-based thinkers. Abundance-based thinkers believe there is enough to go around for everyone and live with a positive, serving mindset. In contrast, fear-based thinkers emphasize an "us vs. them" mentality, believe what's ours needs to be theirs, and feel they must conquer and win at all costs. They believe we must lose in order for them to succeed.

Having a like-minded inner circle ensures they understand who we are. They also must believe all of our dreams and desires are 100% achievable if we make the right choices and take the right actions.

Our inner circle must also value continuous growth and betterment of themselves and those they surround themselves with. Another requirement (and I see this time and time again): they cannot be jealous of our journey and success. They want to see us rise as far in life as we can, even if it surpasses them.

For example, Chris Tuff and I are in each other's inner circles. I don't care if he makes one dollar or ten trillion dollars. I do not care if he becomes more famous than me; I just want him to be ridiculously successful and happy because I love him and know he's making a massive impact in this world. I'm also the first person to kick him in the face if he strays from his core values, and he does the same for me.

It's natural for us to absorb the thoughts and energy of our inner circles. If we continuously hear how bad the world is, especially from those we surround ourselves with, we'll begin believing the world is bad and only seeing the negative around us. If our boards speak with a victim mentality, a sense of entitlement, or constant fear, we'll end up with the same. Pain loves to attract and surround itself with pain!

We must distance ourselves from negative people—all of them, including certain family members and friends. (More on that later.) This might sound cold but—trust me—it isn't. Friends either lift us up or tear us down, and it's 100% up to us to pick who we surround ourselves with. This doesn't mean we don't love them and hope for the best for them. We just don't need negative people around us and certainly not on our personal board of directors.

Instead, my board includes people who love me, hold me accountable, and see through my B.S. and excuses. I open up to them about my struggles, insecurities, fears, and crazy thoughts (the inner critic we all have). Due to our trust, I'm also able to share my failures and large personal mistakes when I deviate from my personal core values.

There are no true failures, by the way. Failures and mistakes are always opportunities to learn and be better. These open communications allow my inner circle to guide me in the appropriate direction—or kick *me* in the proverbial face when needed.

If I call my inner circle at 3 A.M., they'll answer. If I'm stuck on a desert island, they'll rescue me. They know I would do the same for them, too—always! One of our Breedlove household slogans is "We show up!" Another is "Protect and defend this fort!" My inner circle honors these war cries and holds me accountable to them as well.

Our Inner Circles Will Evolve

Our inner circle might start very small. We might have only one person we respect and trust, and that's A-okay. We don't relax our standards just to have more people on our board. I'd rather have one ideal person than 10 mediocre members. It's truly quality over quantity. As we continue to implement the actions from this book, your inner circle will grow, and as a result, so will you—100 times. I promise! Mine has grown continuously since I started my path toward making *me* my full-time job, mastering my mindset, and serving others.

Important: It's crucial that we also always work on our relationships and communication with our significant other. Because they *will* be on the board! In fact, they will be the second-most important member—the Co-Chair, if you will. Heather is my Chief of Staff and I also affectionately call her Management.

When I began, I only had a few people who made it through the filter. The more I dove into gratitude, service, and truly loving those around me, the more my network, income, and relationships (including my inner circle) leveled up. It's truly amazing to see the epic people who show up in our lives when we do this work. It's almost as if our presence, words, and actions start attracting the same type of people and repelling the bad influences. What I saw as success in life years ago compared to what I see now is a million times different. This is because I no longer surround myself with people who limit their own success by believing they have to conquer and win at the expense of everyone else.

We must be super proactive about who we allow into our life. People who we trust one day might not be people whose influence we would want later on in our Legendary journey. This isn't a matter of ego or becoming self-absorbed. We constantly grow and change. So do our goals. It's easy to stay where we are and keep doing the same things over and over, but true change takes massive courage and constant evaluation. We see the world differently as we learn more about ourselves and others. We might remain friends with people who were once in our inner circles, but we need new influences, advice, direction, and support as we evolve.

By choice, I no longer spend time with most of the people I knew from childhood and college. I'm Facebook friends with most of them and enjoy seeing their pictures and watching them live their lives. However, our goals, aspirations, and values are not the same anymore. I have only one remaining friend from my pre-20 days I still spend time with: Ryan Hopkins. Ryan is a mountain of a man in every way, and I still visit him on a regular basis. (Seriously, he is *enormous* and has a massive personality to boot. See the "Incredible Hulk.")

I cannot imagine growing apart from Ryan because he's always working at being a better man, father, and husband every day of his life. We have some of the most raw, honest, and beautiful conversations. We talk about and dissect our failures and triumphs. We love helping each other achieve betterment and constant growth, which have become prerequisites to being in my inner circle.

Everything changes, but too many people *choose not* to change because it's hard and scary. I love being around people who are willing to look in the mirror, see themselves honestly, and work hard to be better. It's so critically important for us to become aware of our strengths, weaknesses, fears, insecurities, and do something about them in order to be the best people we can be.

I don't call this work self-improvement or self-development. I call this work a revelation. We are revealing who we were truly born to be!

Energy Vampires

It's simple: If you want to take action, stay far, far away from people who drain your energy. Ancient literature and modern experts call these people "energy vampires." We must cut energy vampires from our lives as soon as possible and be careful of who we include in our inner circles. My inner circle includes people who are far from perfect, but none of them are energy vampires. They are all extremely positive people on a consistent path to personal improvement—people like you, reading and applying the information in this book to build Legendary lives.

Again, we must absolutely eliminate the energy vampires and the negative people not just from our inner circle but from our lives in general. We all have those people in our lives. We know the ones. The people who walk into the room and all of the energy in our body seems to literally be sucked out in an instant. We shrink or immediately feel the desire to run out of the room.

Vampires come in various forms including but not limited to these:
- the victim
- the "I need to dominate" person
- the drama queen
- the judger, and
- the Me Monsters

The Me Monsters' favorite topic to discuss is themselves! When you have a moment, watch Brian Regan's hilarious comedy bit on the Me Monsters. It is *epic*, and you're welcome in advance!

Finally, we must remember the people we allow to speak most frequently into our lives are ourselves. We must watch out for negative self-talk—the internal critic who tells us we aren't good enough, smart enough, handsome enough, thin enough, or whatever. The ultimate Energy Vampire.

As the chair of our personal board of directors, we need to silence our internal critic. If we would not permit someone else to speak to us like that, we must not allow our inner critic to, either. One of my mentors, Kerry Geho, had a hilarious but very powerful saying: "Don't make fun of me. That's my job!" Being truthful to ourselves means being honest about areas for improvement *and* all the good things about us. The vast majority of the time, negative self-talk is a bunch of lies based on shame and fears given to us by others.

Throughout this book, I share tactics for handling our inner critic. One amazing way to do this is to respond to the inner critic as if we were another person, as a study published in 2019 in *Psychology Today* suggested.[3] For example, if my inner critic says I'm "too emotional" sometimes, I can pause and say, "Tommy, you've come this far because you've chosen to be yourself. So don't be afraid to call people beautiful humans, talk about love and abundance, or practice daily affirmations." (Just FYI, we affectionately named my self-critic Ike. I laugh at him now when he gets loud. However, it has taken years of hard work and implementing the practices within this book to silence my old buddy Ike!)

Setting Strong Family Boundaries

"If you look around your family and do not see the crazy one, you're it!" It's a great joke, but more often than not, it's oh so true. We all have people in our families who frustrate us to no end. They are filled with negativity, complain about everything imaginable, and work at guilting and shaming us to death.

---

3 "Silencing Your Inner Critic." Psychology Today. Sussex Publishers. Accessed November 1, 2019. https://www.psychologytoday.com/us/articles/201903/silencing-your-inner-critic.

We love our family members and want the best for them, but no matter what we say or do, nothing changes. We know they could have a better life if they made a few simple changes. Every Thanksgiving dinner, however, it's the same complaining and negativity for many of us.

This cycle is especially tough on people looking to build and live Legendary lives. When we invest so much time and emotional energy to help people we love make better choices, we become *really* exhausted. It's because we can *only* change ourselves and nobody else, not even our families. We can love, influence, and guide them if they are willing, but *they must choose to change and take action* in order for them to find peace, happiness, and success in life.

We must set strong boundaries with negative family members. We cannot control what they do or shoulder the burdens of their poor choices. Sometimes boundaries mean spending less time with them. (Some in my family say *I* am the crazy one! Yes, I love it! That means I'm winning on the ole' setting-proper-boundaries front.)

"Setting boundaries with family still means loving them—but taking action to stop the inappropriate behaviors."

I made the tough choice recently to no longer speak to a close family member of mine who lives on a dangerous path. This person has refused to get help or better their life despite my reaching out multiple times. I decided to cut off all communication when the texts coming in were continuously angry, hateful, and full of jealousy. Even though I've set this strong boundary, I continue to feel compassion toward them and pray they'll find peace and choose to take action to change their life for the better.

This is an extreme example, but it illustrates the importance of boundaries. My life has been directly happier as a result. We might not need to cut off communication, but to become Legendary, we need to be able to love family members from afar at times. If we wouldn't choose them to be on our board of directors, we must not let them influence us as if they were. We can love them all. We can see them on major holidays—or not. We cannot improve their lives, however. Only they can.

Are we cold, insensitive, and unresponsive when we choose to spend less time with people who are not positive influences in our lives? Other people can believe this, but we must protect and defend this fort. Cutting off ties is also never my first move. My first, second, third, and—depending on my relationship with the person—one-hundredth move is *always* to do everything in my power to lift them up. Eventually, I realize I've done everything in my power to help, and I pull back. It doesn't mean I don't love them. I love them all, I really do. I just don't want to be around people who are not taking action to be better than they were yesterday. I choose to step away from others who take away my energy and happiness.

Hire Slow, Fire Fast

In business, many of us live by this mantra. Hiring slow helps protect our businesses by making it harder for poor fits to get hired. If a poor fit makes it through, firing them quickly is better for everyone. It helps them to find a more appropriate job based on their skill sets and protects our business from them negatively influencing other team members.

The same holds true for our relationships. I used to be terrible at hiring slow and firing fast as I wanted to trust and love everybody. People, even certain "close" friends, just kept taking advantage of me especially with picking my brain without ever reciprocating in return. So, go slowly with any new relationship. Don't go all-in at first. I have been burned *sooo* many times by going all-in way too soon!

Let's learn people's true colors before we allow them to become close to us. I love taking new acquaintances to dinner to see how they treat the wait staff. This is a trick I learned in the business world to see whom to work with and, more importantly, *not* to work with, including clients. I have zero tolerance for people who are rude to waiters or, for that matter, any other person serving us or making our lives easier or better. If someone is rude to the people who serve us, they'll be rude to anybody. (Common sense check-in: Restaurant employees control the safety, taste, and quality of our food; why would we ever want to be rude to these truly powerful people?)

It takes massive courage to take action and fire someone close to us. Honestly, though, it will be better for everyone. Chances are, both sides are frustrated. Let's choose to end it in the right way with love and grace. Over time, we can graciously distance ourselves from them and the events we once attended together. Eventually, nature will take its course, the relationship will end, and we'll all have space in our lives for something even better.

Ultimately, our inner circles have a massive impact on our lives, and vice versa. As we change our actions, thoughts, and mindsets, a positive force passes between us and our closest confidants, increasing success all around. My inner circle and I have been humbled and blessed to experience so much business and life success by showing up for each other, holding each other accountable, and ultimately having a burning desire to ensure we all are truly the best humans we can be.

LEGENDARY ACTIONS & REMINDERS

- Begin building a personal board of directors or inner circle for your life. Start with people you trust, give you rock-solid advice, and truly want the best for you. Important: We *must* do the same for them.
- Take regular inventory of your inner circle. Do adjustments need to be made, and do members need to be hired or fired?
- Hire slow and fire fast. Take small, incremental steps with any new relationship. Remember that positive action comes from positive interactions. See how potential inner circle members treat service people; if it's poorly, run the other way.
- If you do nothing else, eliminate all of the energy vampires from your life.

Chapter 8

Blocking Out the Noise

Cade Joiner, who's part of my inner circle and an epic human, began his Legendary journey while riding the D.C. Metro—but not in the way you might think.

Let's go back in time a moment. Straight out of college, Cade worked on Capitol Hill, doing incredible things, including attending high-level meetings in the White House. He was living his lifelong dream, or so he thought. After four months, Cade began becoming overwhelmed by all of the noise—media, drama, and, of course, politics. It was completely wearing him down.

One weekend at a bookstore, Cade began flipping through *Entrepreneur* magazine and read about Greg Brophy, who had a very successful Canadian business called Shred-It. He suddenly realized he could do something similar in the U.S. He grabbed a café napkin and a pen and began jotting down notes to devise his plan of attack. Later, back home, he drafted a business plan but tucked it away in a drawer, unsure what to do next.

The noise surrounding Cade continued so often that he found himself praying one day on the D.C. Metro: "*Lord, I need you to give me a sign of what I need to do."* When Cade exited the subway and rode up the escalator to the street, he saw the sign he was seeking. It was none other than one of Greg Brophy's shredding trucks. Immediately, Cade knew *that moment* was the time to start his own shredding business, which is exactly what he did.

The business has been so successful it has allowed Cade to return to politics on his terms, become a very impactful investor, and to spend significant amounts of quality time with his beautiful family. This is what I call living Legendary, ladies and gentlemen!

> "People don't think about you that much, so don't be worried about what they're thinking."
> —Cade Joiner

Cade tells me he wouldn't have been able to be so successful in life and business without blocking out all of society's noise. "You have to be like a horse with blinders—block out all of the distractions," he says. "I simply don't care about what other people are doing or thinking. If you're afraid to fail because you don't want people to call you an idiot, then you're never going to go anywhere or amount to anything. You'll never move forward. People don't think about you that much, so don't be worried about what they're thinking."

Noise is the death of all things compassion, courage, love, and integrity. Just watch national news or a politician for two minutes—noise!

Blocking out the noise begins with understanding what the noise is and then putting on our blinders and earplugs. In this chapter, we'll also discuss the importance of shutting down jealousy and envy while discovering new ways to get more in tune with the wise inner voice that always knows what to do next.

If we simply block out even 50% of the noise, we'll feel better, our mindset will improve, and we'll have more compassion for others. I hope you find this chapter as massively important as I do. Be prepared. This is the only "negative and potentially overwhelming" chapter in the book, and it is intended to be that way. Fasten your seat belts, my fellow Legends in the making!

What Is Noise?

All the distractions in life keeping us from living our purpose, truly being ourselves, and following our passions are noise.

Noise is (but not limited to):

- 24-hour news
- The opinions of others
- Social media
- Reality TV
- Gossip TV
- Politics of any kind
- The aggressiveness of large cities in the name of "progress"
- Pornography—a killer of our relationships, romance, and intimacy
- Video games
- Cell phones
- Newspapers
- Radical and condemning religious leaders
- Email
- Celebrity magazines
- Negative, jealous, and judging humans we associate with

Where Is Noise Found?

Unfortunately, *everywhere*! Look no further than the nightly news or your social media feed and you will be inundated with noise. Our media and society crave tragic and fear-inducing stories. Don't get me wrong; I'm super empathetic to the needs of our fellow humans worldwide. However, some people have fetishized sad and scary stories to the point where we *must* tune out.

Our fictional TV shows are also full of manipulation, aggression, darkness, and hopelessness. Based on our watching habits, it appears we crave watching others fail, fall, or die. Why, I wonder? Could it be because we do not feel good or believe in ourselves enough, so we want the worst for others? I hope not and if so, this book will certainly help undo that false wiring in our hearts and brains.

Then there are our cities. Most of us who spend more than a day in Las Vegas are completely exhausted for a reason. Developers have intentionally built Vegas using every temptation imaginable to take up our time, energy, money, and destroy our morals in the name of a "good time." It truly is Sin City, from the lights, incessant noise, partying, and indecent ads every 20 feet to the "What happens in Vegas stays in Vegas" catchphrase. (This motto is basically just a clever way of saying, "I'm going to destroy my value system for three days in the name of fun and to fit in and hopefully be liked by traveling mates.") Noise, my friends—*noise*!

I have been as guilty as the next person of falling prey to it all. And note, I still go to Vegas once or twice a year, but I spend more time at shows, hiking, and in restaurants these days. I just cannot take the noise and watch my fellow beautiful humans succumb to all of the darkness. By day two, I'm completely drained from the sensory overload.

So What Does Noise Do to Us?
"Noise makes us angry, envious, judgmental, insecure, jealous, apathetic, lazy, and scared!"

It makes total sense: garbage in equals garbage out. If we constantly put the garbage of 24-hour news, reality TV, gossip, and negative social media into our hearts, minds, and souls, garbage thinking from us is going to make its way into our work, lives, and relationships.

Worst of all, noise causes us to crave the approval of others. Ugh! We all fall into the trap of judging, envy, and compromising to be accepted by our tribe. Me, too! It takes one to know one, trust me. When I watch even a few minutes of the news or scroll through my social, I'm super aware of the judgment, anger, and envy that arises in others and in me. I can literally feel it in my shoulders and chest. This also wears me out mentally and emotionally, and most of us are numb to the fact it's happening.

Designers have intentionally created social media, phones, most apps, and video games to be psychologically addictive. In fact, recent studies have shown these "behavioral addictions" are likely to have the same symptoms and withdrawal effects as heroin. I repeat, designers want us addicted to the pain and noise—*UGH!*

Blocking Out the Noise (and the News)

We want to stop tuning into the news, our phones, and social media—but society won't let us, and the truth is, we won't. Pain truly loves pain.

My friends, it's totally up to us to take our goodness and power back from all of this noise. If we turn off the TV, put the phone down, and step up and into our lives, we just might enjoy

- an amazing conversation with a friend
- actually watching and experiencing an event through our eyes and not our phones
- feeling better about ourselves
- reconnecting intimately and romantically with the people we love

---

"I have chosen to no longer compromise my emotional and mental health with poisonous media. The news, as it stands now, has the sole purpose of dividing us and scaring us. Unfortunately, the "us vs. them" mentality and "fear" is what sells. Period! It's time to tune it out and be of service to ourselves and those closest to us. If we concentrate on being better than we were yesterday and serving our fellow humans, our world would be a dramatically different place."

A Rest Day

Here's a super difficult challenge for you. Are you up for it? Do you have what it takes? We shall see!

Take one day a week off from social media, your phone, video games, TV, computer, and news. If you truly desire to be happy and peaceful, take a sabbatical day from *all* of them!

While taking this challenge, notice how your hands start shaking and you crave and need the electronics after only a few minutes. How many times do you feel the urge to grab your heroin, oops, sorry about that, I mean your phone?

If you are able to conquer this challenge, and I totally believe you can, even though it is sooooo freaking hard, you will notice an exponential improvement to your happiness and peace of mind. Case in point: my team member Lindsey completely eliminated her Facebook newsfeed and said it has massively impacted her life for the better.

Please let me know how you do with this challenge. It will be one of the toughest things you ever do.

Our brains and hearts are our most important organs, and we must refuse to allow them to be polluted with negative information and the opinions of others. The noise will keep us from doing our best work, living our best lives, and making an impact.

When some of my heroes said they felt happier and more productive in their everyday lives by simply turning off the news, I decided to block it out, too. I've modified my social media feeds to block negative pages and friends (you know who you are). I now see only uplifting posts, and it makes a huge difference. I now have a zero news policy. I also keep my phone on "Do Not Disturb" for major portions of the day.

In *The Four-Hour Workweek* (an epic book, by the way) my boy Tim Ferris offers sage advice on blocking out the news. Tim says if it's important enough, everybody's going to be talking about it, so you're going to get the important news from the people around you anyway. So why watch it in the first place? Genius, and you know what? He's so freaking right!

After the fourth person asked about my opinion on the Brett Kavanaugh hearings, I wondered who he was and why he might be relevant to me or anyone else for that matter. So I made a phone call: "Mom, who's Kavanaugh, and why is everybody talking about him?" I had no idea. None, *nada*, zero. She said, "Tommy, you weren't kidding, you really don't watch the news." Note—as I write this sentence, no one has mentioned the guy's name to me in six months. Point made!

Sometimes, people believe I am foolish or completely uninformed when I tell them I don't watch the news, but it's paid more dividends to my peace of mind than anything else outside of gratitude and meditation. Certain friends have become annoyed because I won't sit around and talk about Republicans, Democrats, who cheated on whom, and other judgy news topics. I'd rather make time for more interesting conversations with my friends' lives. What cool things are they working toward? What are their dreams? What are they learning? Who would they fight for and why?

My life is more meaningful simply because I won't have superficial, empty conversations anymore about other people, celebrity gossip, or politics. Because of this change, I'm not nearly as angry or worried as I used to be and am now happier than ever.

Truth Bomb: I do still love my conversations around sports, especially as they pertain to my beloved Georgia Bulldogs; and the Atlanta Braves, Hawks, Falcons, and United. Yes, I am a hometown boy through and through! This is one of my guilty pleasures and vices to this day and will be until my last breath. I believe sports unite communities and can make us so happy and sad in all of the right ways.

P.S. GO DAWGS!!

No Noise, New Vision

I participated in an 11-day vision quest ceremony with Kedar Brown, a nature-based ceremonialist and shamanic healer. He has become a good friend and a great mentor in my life.

Talk about blocking out the noise. I had only my thoughts, fears, insecurities, and a whole lot of discomfort during my alone time in the North Carolina mountains. For four full days and nights, I was in the wilderness with no tent, no phone, no books, no humans, no food:

nothing. In other words, no distractions. Just me, my soul, thoughts, fears, and God. It was a really scary place to be—even aside from the snakes, spiders, ants, and bears. The quest was designed to be a death and rebirth ceremony where I let the worst part of me die—literally.

I chose the vision quest to face my demons and past, to let go, and to forgive but never forget. I also worked through memories to figure out which ones were true or untrue. I looked my angers and fears square in the face. It was a profoundly challenging and beautiful experience. The final three days of the program were the rebirth, where Kedar and the other counselors gave me the tools, skills, and systems to enter back into society with a newfound sense of peace.

Immediately when I returned home, and against all of the vision quest counselors' recommendations, I headed straight into an entrepreneurial conference. Oops! It was unreal. I was super aware of my thoughts and feelings and because of this, the conference was unlike anything I had ever experienced.

It's hard to explain or quantify and might seem like hocus pocus, but I felt like I could see right through the facades, armor, and fakeness people were wearing and right into their souls of who they really are. I could see their insecurities and masks—the characters and roles they were playing vs. who they really were. It was almost unbearable for three or four days. Because of this, my transition back was far from graceful, but overall, it was a profound experience.

We all have deep wounds, and they will not heal until we bring them into the light. When we don't do the hard work, when we continue to sweep our fears and pasts under the rug, they will continue to haunt us in many ways from relationships to jobs to friendships. For me, this was just one more step in a long journey of rebuilding and ideally, becoming Legendary one day.

I realize that going on a vision quest is an extreme example of getting away from the noise. However, I do encourage all of us to start doing something to step away from the TV, phones, and media, and to work on ourselves.

Organized retreats are another great way to block out the noise. Right now, I'm considering attending a 10-day silent meditation retreat recently recommended by my friend Colin O'Brady. (Look him up. He is a straight-up physical specimen and the holder of many extreme sports world records.) During a dinner with Colin and some members of my inner circle, he shared how attending silent retreats is the most impactful thing he does to train his mind, get ready for a world-record climb, and to get in touch with his soul. He eliminates the noise and gets completely in tune with his body, inner thoughts, and fears. It allows him to do mind-blowing accomplishments and inspire millions! If it's good enough for Colin, it's good enough for me.

Jealousy and Envy

Noise can be silent, too: just look at jealousy and envy. I represent a lot of high-wealth clients who have done very well in business. They're highly respected members of society who also live in huge homes and drive nice cars. It's easy to be envious of their lives, not understanding the burden they carry. However, I've learned how luxury is never enough. These clients usually come to me to seek peace, be better parents and spouses, and ultimately to find happiness and fulfillment in what seemed like the perfect life.

What people don't realize is the more successful you are, the less time you have, and the higher the burdens are, such as more employees, responsibilities, businesses, and assets to protect. In fact, some of my wealthiest clients carry the burden of thousands of lives by the decisions they make within their business. They are amazing humans who take this burden very seriously, regardless of what the haters say about them.

No matter what our Instagram feed shows us, I have a friendly reminder for us all: not one single person on this Earth is perfect, and we are all scared and insecure regardless of how we look on the outside. Here's a second friendly reminder: we all use the bathroom, we all get sick, and we all eventually will die and become worm food. Thus, we all have the same fate in the end, so why be jealous and envious during our short time here?

Jealousy and envy are diseases of the mind and soul. They cause us to become angry, scared, insecure, judge others, and spend money we don't have to impress people we don't like. Social media and celebrity gossip talk shows have one intention, to make us judgmental and jealous. Finally, the saddest and most dangerous person in the world is a jealous person. I know, I've been there, and what a horrible sight it was to behold.

Here's a tactic for us to implement. Instead of being envious and jealous, let's celebrate each other's wins and lift each other up in goodness. When we become envious of someone else's success, take a quick moment and ask ourselves why. In that question lies our deepest desires and fears.

When we root for people to fail and collapse, suffering always come back to us tenfold. However, the reverse is also true! When we want those around us to be truly successful, well, you guessed it: success will also certainly follow us. Replacing envy with celebration will have a profound impact on becoming the master of our thoughts and ultimately our destinies.

Here's to us cutting out the noise, beautiful humans!

LEGENDARY ACTIONS & REMINDERS

- What's a source of noise you're willing to minimize or eliminate from your life? Start by committing to only one hour a day. Ask an accountability partner to help you implement this into your life.

- Write this truth where you can see it regularly: Garbage in equals garbage out. If you watch negative news, you'll become negative. If you scroll through somebody's angry and judgmental Facebook page, you'll become angry and judgmental yourself. Pain truly loves more pain!
- Challenge: Take an electronics sabbatical at least one day a week. During this day, do not look at your phone, TV, computer, or other distractions. Notice how difficult this is and the withdrawal symptoms you experience. Let me know how long you actually make it.
- Attend a nature or silent retreat, which will force you to block out the noise.
- Remember that jealousy and envy are noise and diseases of the soul and mind. Nobody on this Earth is perfect, and we are all scared and insecure.
- If you do nothing else, reread this chapter and educate others on how hidden sources of noise are manipulating us, and why it's so important to take our lives and power back into our own hands.

Chapter 9

Mastering Our Mindset

"Tommy, I'm not so sure about this."

I'll never forget the day my dear friend Darrah Brustein approached me with some serious doubts about her upcoming project. A successful entrepreneur and a world-class networker, Darrah has exemplified taking action and living and working with passion and purpose throughout her amazing rise to the top of the business world. *Why*, I thought, *would she have any doubts? Darrah's a true legend in the making!*

Darrah's goal was to stage a massive virtual summit, which she'd never done before. The idea came from a series of conversations with her inner circle where she asked questions like:

- "What's something you think I don't know about myself?"
- "When do you think I'm at my best?" and
- "When do you think I'm at my worst?"

First of all, asking epic questions like those takes courage, beautiful humans—straight up intestinal fortitude. If you really want to take a good hard look in the mirror. Ask your close friends when you're at your worst. Most of the time, what we see in the mirror and what others see in us is . . . very different.

Answers in hand, Darrah began crafting her virtual summit, which she called "Life By Design, Not By Default." The doubts, however, continued, and she began to ask herself, "What if I fail publicly?"

Instead of giving up, Darrah took the steps to master her mindset and silence her inner critic, took action, and even harder—finished!

Life By Design, Not By Default was a tremendous success, to say the least. To date, Darrah's had more than 10,000 people attend her virtual summit and booked such speakers as Deepak Chopra and Adam Grant. I've heard story after story of the positive impact her summit has had on people all over the world. If Darrah had failed to master her mindset and given into the fears, the world would have missed out on a very inspiring event.

Just like Darrah, we can become the masters of our own mindset and minimize that inner voice saying, "We are not good enough." Before we learn how, let's discuss that terrible monster known as perfectionism.

Perfectionism—A Killer!

Whether setting a goal, moving in a new direction, or making a big decision, it's natural for doubt and fear to seep into our thinking. Also, for us ambitious types, we are always on a relentless pursuit of this unattainable thing called perfection. Perfection kills our ability to take our first giant step toward anything new or better, to continue to take action after starting, and even worse, to finish!

We've spent our entire lives as high achievers wanting to be in the game, competing, winning, and eventually conquering. What happens if we fall short and are less than—well, you guessed it—perfect? Sadly, a lot of us never get started, or we quit, or, worse, stop just short of finishing our goal.

As we discussed earlier, social media also amplifies our desires to be all things perfect. Even if we're pros at blocking out the noise, the numerous images of perfect people, perfect vacations, and perfect lives creep their way into our hearts and minds inch by inch.

There's great news, my fellow Legends in the making! There is an antidote to perfectionism. As I will say time and time again—all we have to do is take action! As the great James Victore writes in *Feck Perfuction*, inspiration without action is B.S. and vice versa.

By following the steps in this chapter and throughout this book, we will understand how *done* is *always* better than perfect. We will know perfection is unattainable and, even better, we will not care as we will be focusing on action, purpose, and impact.

We will let go of our fears, insecurities, and mental anchors holding us back. We will stop looking backward into the past because we will become so excited about the present. We will learn not to fear the future because we will be positioned to make the greatest impact for ourselves and others—right here and right now!

It's time to seize this day and master our mindsets, my friends! Let's take action by practicing meditation and gratitude, visualizing, and rewiring our brains to get rid of the fear and find abundance.

Visualization

An incredible story from the amazing career of Michael Phelps explains how visualization is one of the great keys to mastering our mindset. In August 2008, at the Beijing Olympic Games, Phelps was about to swim the last leg of the men's 200-meter relay. Victory was in sight—or was it? Just as he dove in, his goggles filled with water, and the crisis only grew worse throughout the race. Eventually, Phelps could not see at all and was swimming blind. Something amazing happened, however. Incredibly, Phelps became *faster* as his visibility worsened— eventually winning the race and breaking his own world record by 0.06

seconds. Why? Because Phelps had practiced that race a thousand times prior in his head. He had visualized every stroke of his Olympic swim including winning the race, leaving no chance for failure. His mind and body were prepared—he knew exactly where to flip, when to breathe, and how to win!

Anytime I have a big public talk or something important to prepare for, I always do a visualization exercise. I turn off my phone and other sources of noise and get completely quiet. In my mind, I walk myself through the entire event or speech. I see the audience and mentally watch their responses and reactions to what I am saying. I imagine all my actions and pauses. I smell, feel, and experience every detail. This prepares my mind and body for what *could* happen and how I *want* it to happen.

I always have my clients prepare and practice a visualization exercise anytime they ask for a raise or promotion, have a difficult conversation with a spouse or child, or prepare for anything they deem important. This tactic is truly a game changer.

Spend 10 to 30 minutes before the next big meeting, interview, tough conversation, or event practicing how you'll achieve your goal. You will be shocked at how well you perform.

The Power of Meditation

Meditation is one of the most powerful tools in helping us become the master over our thoughts and emotions. Meditation is exercise for our brains and souls. My life has changed in so many incredible ways by meditating less than 20 minutes a day.

This simple act is the single best way for us to be more proactive as opposed to reactive to the world's challenges. Through consistent meditation practice, we begin to think before we speak or react, pause, breathe, and when the time is appropriate, respond with the best solution. When we're proactive in our lives, we become the masters of our situations and not the servant of them.

Meditation also helps keep us in the here and now and fully present with others. When we are fully present and engaged with others, our listening and leadership skills become extraordinary. Others notice when we're fully present and our relationships improve dramatically. Being fully present in our conversations is a rarity these days and will set us apart from others who are constantly planning their next move.

It can feel extremely difficult at first and, like anything worth undertaking, takes consistency, patience, and time before we can reap the benefits. I call it going to the mental gym. We have to work out consistently to lose weight and get fit. The same goes for rewiring our brains. The key is not to judge when we realize our minds are constantly racing. I've been meditating for nearly a decade, and sometimes my mind will only be silent for 10 to 45 seconds at a time. However, when my mind is silent only for a fleeting moment, the peace and stillness are magnificent.

Great meditations I recommend are the Calm app, all of the Oprah Winfrey and Deepak Chopra 21 Day Meditation Challenges, the Headspace app, and anything from Wayne Dyer.

I have also created a meditation series for ambitious, driven people to help us get focused and ready to seize the day! Check it out at TommyBreedlove.com/Legendary!

Everything Happens *for* Us Rather Than *to* Us

Instead of quitting, both Darrah Brustein and Michael Phelps overcame their negative thoughts to make the most of their situations. Both have also expressed gratitude for how their difficult circumstances allowed them to be at their best. To put it another way, broken goggles didn't happen *to* Phelps, they happened *for* Phelps, making him even more world class. He is one human that I can say with complete certainty is truly a Legend.

When we reframe our mindsets from a "Why is this happening *to* me?" (victim) mentality, to a "Why is this happening *for* me?" (learnings), we move from a fear and scarcity mentality to the wonderful place of gratitude and abundance. Instead of being victims or martyrs, we become appreciative students. We see the learnings and goodness in every situation, even the terrible ones! This is the power of gratitude and perspective, my beautiful humans. Gratitude always allows us to be present, right here and right now, and appreciate what we do have and not lament what we don't have.

For example, when get stuck in traffic, we can either get mad and cowardly honk the horn at people we don't know — or ask ourselves, "Why is this happening for me?" Maybe the traffic prevents me from being in a car wreck down the road. Maybe it gives us time to call an old friend or loved one; or a moment of quiet meditation in our car; or time to listen to our favorite book (*this* book of course, right?).

Do you see how powerful it is shifting from anger, frustration, and entitlement to gratitude for the extra time? When we do this, we begin rewiring our brains and eventually believing life is happening *for* us rather than *to* us.

This is truly game changing when life *really* gets difficult—business losses, family sickness, relationship troubles, etc. Having the "for me" attitude looks at the lessons in every failure, loss, or tragedy. This attitude allows us to see the learning and opportunities for growth in everything. *When*, not *if*, the next tough business or life event happens, we'll be more ready and powerful than before as we have learned and embraced the difficulties from the past.

Remember, everything in our lives—and I mean *everything*—happens *for* us rather than *to* us. Think about a situation in your past when something went wrong or someone was hurting you. What lesson in life has it taught you? What happens to your peace of mind and attitude when you flip the scenario from a victim mindset to a learning and gratitude mindset? For me, this slight shift in my thinking was a game changer!

Our Thoughts Create Our Outcomes

In Chapter 8, I shared some lessons I learned about blocking out the noise during my 11-day vision quest. While I was starving, scared, and in complete isolation from other humans, I also learned a lot about the power of my thoughts during that retreat.

The experience reinforced my discovery of how brains are like our muscles—the stronger they are, the stronger we can be. I also learned how we can positively influence so much of our lives by changing the way we think, especially about ourselves. Our thoughts influence the world around us, including money, love, friendships, and business networks.

As the great Kedar Brown taught me, "Be mindful of your thoughts, because they are your prayers."

For example, If Darrah *really* thought she would fail at her virtual summit, she would have. She would have self-sabotaged by quitting or giving less than her full effort. By shifting her thoughts back to the positive, taking action, and pouring herself into the project, Darrah triumphed. *Our thoughts create our outcomes.* It is a self-fulfilling prophecy. When we become the master of our thoughts and think positively and abundantly while minimizing the fear, we have massively positive results in our business and personal lives.

"Whether you think you can or you can't, you're right."
—Henry Ford

Can't is another one of those dirty, filthy, nasty words, like *impossible*, *try*, *busy*, and *should*. I've also eliminated the word *can't* from my vocabulary. *Can't* is the birthplace of "I won't do that," and you know what, beautiful humans? "I won't go there."

Even today, after numerous years of working on my mental and emotional fortress, I still sometimes catch my thoughts heading in a negative direction. Thank goodness I catch them much sooner now, but it still happens. That evil self-critic is always lingering. Like visualization and meditation, one of our primary and quite possibly the most powerful weapons in the war to conquer our mindsets is gratitude.

The Impact of Gratitude

For me, practicing gratitude has been the single most beneficial skill I have developed in my pursuit of becoming Legendary.

When we look at what we're thankful for, we are immediately taken to the present moment and transformed from a place of fear or anger to a place of love and abundance.

For the haters who believe saying "thank you" can't change our lives, let's take a look at the amazing proof. In his book, *The Code of the Extraordinary Mind*, which I *highly* recommend, Vishen Lakhiani discusses the scientifically proven benefits of even a small practice. Vishen explains how people who simply wrote down five things they are thankful for from the previous week showed a 25% increase in happiness.

Who doesn't want to be 25% happier?

Vishen discovered people with an active gratitude practice also exercise more, feel healthier, and experience "more energy, forgiving attitudes, less depression, fewer headaches, better sleep, more feelings of being socially connected, and less anxiousness."

Whew, another mouthful, but who doesn't need more of all that goodness in their lives?

I love the following from Vishen's book: "Apparently gratitude leads to giving, which in turn boosts the happiness and gratitude of others. That's the kind of social contagion I can get behind."

Me, too, my brother. Me, too!

Gratitude has also been proven to open the doors to better relationships, enhanced empathy, reduced aggression, improved self-esteem, and increased mental strength. Do I have your attention, my beautiful humans?

Practicing Gratitude

Gratitude requires discipline and daily practice, and when we talk about becoming Legendary, it all begins and ends with this. To repeat, it is the most life-changing skill I have implemented in my life. Remember, we are building tough mental muscles. Just like going to the gym, over time, we will see the benefits of gratitude throughout all phases of our lives. The benefits will be peace of mind, being proactive and not reactive in our lives, increased happiness, and attracting other like-minded abundance-filled people.

Are you ready to regain your power and become the master of your mindset? If so, let's go!

Practice One—Starting the Day with a Positive Mindset

The first thing we think about when waking up sets the tone for the rest of the day. Therefore, let's start our days by being thankful.

Side note – We can set a wake-up alarm or ringtone that is peaceful and does not make every hair on our head stand up or our dogs howl. As soon as we open our eyes, let's take a moment and say, "Thank you for allowing me to serve this day." Then we can think about one positive thing we "get to do" that day. Boom. Now we're on the positive train!

As we stand up from our beds, we can say "thank you" as each foot touches the floor. Finally, as we walk to the restroom, let's say "thank you" with each step.

Welcome to beginning your day in goodness and abundance. We *get* to live our lives today! Does it really get any better than that?

Practice Two—Journaling with Gratitude

Each morning, I spend 90 minutes to two hours working on my mental, emotional, physical, and spiritual health so I may serve others in the best way possible. As part of this routine, in a special journal I use for affirmations and appreciation, I write five things I am grateful for. Examples include, "I am so happy and grateful for:

- the unconditional love of my wife Heather."
- the beating of my heart and breath in my lungs."
- my desire to be better than I was yesterday and me taking action on this desire."

- my home, friends, and living in a free country."

After I write these five things, I go back and reread them and literally say thank you to each item silently in my head.

IMPORTANT—The list must include gratitude to ourselves for something we have done or said. Over time, this minimizes the impact of that terrible inner critic so we can start noticing all of our wonderful talents and contributions to this world.

Literally, the list is limitless if we just take the time to look around and think of all the things we actually *do* have.

Practice Three—The Game Changer

Are you ready? This one is difficult, takes great self-awareness, and must be practiced throughout every day.

To become self-aware, begin watching your thoughts and emotions throughout the day. Are your thoughts mostly filled with happiness, gratitude, abundance, compassion, and courage? Or are your thoughts mostly filled with fear, anger, envy, jealousy, and judgment? Make it a point to be intentional about watching your emotions throughout the day.

Every time we become angry, impatient, scared, judgmental, or envious of others, we must stop, take one deep breath in and out, and say something we are grateful for in that very moment. It is literally impossible to be angry or insecure when you are grateful. Notice this is the one time I will allow "impossible" into my vocabulary because it's so powerful here. Over time, living in gratitude will become our standard operating mindset. Be patient. This takes time.

To help with this: Throughout the day, say a small "thank you" to everything we appreciate, whether it's your morning cappuccino, a productive meeting, or even just a bird flying overhead. Use a sticky note or calendar reminder so you don't forget. (It's so easy to get caught up in the daily minutiae.)

For me, at first, I literally would force myself to "stop and smell the roses" throughout the day, which has become an amazing way of living. Examples of things I notice and feel thankful for include the blue sky, a pretty flower, police officers who keep us safe and risk their lives every day, or a great phone conversation with a friend. I also silently thank all of my meals and the people who prepare and serve our food. You get the picture.

When you perform this exercise and do not like your state of mind, intentionally shift your thoughts to see good in the world. Be intentional about this. When you look for the good, you will find it.

If you practice nothing else in this book except gratitude, your peace of mind, happiness, and opportunities in life will increase 1,000X.

"If we all implemented a practice of gratitude and small acts of kindness throughout our days, this world would be a remarkable place. The "us vs. them" nonsense would cease to exist. All of us have the power to change this world and make a difference."

Practice Four—Closing our Days with Appreciation

Finally, before closing your eyes, take a moment and tell yourself thank you for giving it your best this day. And then silently think of two or three other items you are grateful for. This will end your day in gratitude and peace of mind to help you sleep well and have pleasant dreams.

Bonus Practices: "A Test of Courage"

Time to man and woman up, my dear friends. If you want to take your marriage or relationship to another level, take a few moments before you switch off the lights at night to look your partner in the eye and say why you're grateful to them. Watch your relationship and sex life soar to all-new levels! This one is very hard to do and takes a lot of courage and vulnerability. Are you up to it? Do you have the coconuts to honor yourself and your partner?

Also, at least once a day, make it a point to tell someone via text, video, phone, or in person how grateful you are for them. Watch your friendships flourish!

Gratitude Is a Way of Life

Our goal is to have gratitude become our standard operating mindset and way of life. It's the most powerful practice to rewire our brains to positivity and silence the inner critic. Over time, seeing the good in the world, operating from a place of love and service, and being thankful for every blessing in our life will be the norm—a lifetime commitment worth honoring.

Oprah Winfrey has a daily practice of gratitude. I can say with certainty she is a legend. She has served millions of people and is happy in life. Oprah says: "When you allow yourself to feel gratitude in the present moment, in the now, what I promise you is the spiritual dimension of your life begins to change. It opens up and expands, and you just grow with it. If you want to change your state of being, start with gratitude."

Man, oh man, I truly love that woman! Her voice nourishes my soul. (Oprah, give me a holler when you have a moment. Seriously.)

LEGENDARY ACTIONS & REMINDERS

- Practice visualization: Spend ten minutes before a meeting, interview, tough conversation, or event rehearsing how you'll achieve your goal.

- Begin and end your day with a short gratitude practice. Watch your days get better and your sleep more restful.

- Every day, in a gratitude journal, write five things you are grateful for. There are no right or wrong entries, it's *your* gratitude.

- Throughout the day, say a small "thank you" to everything you appreciate. Use a sticky note or calendar notification to remind you.

- Begin watching your thoughts and emotions throughout the day. Are they mostly filled with happiness, gratitude, abundance, compassion, and courage? Or are they mostly filled with fear, anger, envy, jealousy, and judgment? When you perform this exercise and do not like your state of mind, shift your thoughts to seeing what is good in the world. Be intentional. When you look for the good, you will find it.

- Step up and step in and tell your spouse something you are thankful for related to them prior to going to sleep. You've got this!

- If you do nothing else, implement the third gratitude practice above, the game changer. Set reminders throughout the day to ensure you build this epically positive habit. Watch your whole life change after just thirty days.

P.S. (Seriously though, someone please have Oprah call me, just so I can say thank you.)

Chapter 10

Living the Good Life

Most of us remember the genius marketing campaign by Dos Equis beer with the most interesting man in the world. The most interesting man in the world did not always drink beer, but when he did, it was Dos Equis—*brilliant*.

In my humble opinion, the most interesting man in the world is my dear friend, Michael Liss. An art major at the University of Georgia (where professors nearly failed him because of his risqué work), Michael is now a very successful international banker based in Shanghai. He's a true pro, the best in the banking business, and a consummate learner who speaks Chinese and Spanish fluently.

Despite his prestigious career, however, Michael refuses to take life too seriously. He pours his spare time into his friendships and living life to the fullest. Michael also knows how to let loose and have an epically good time. I've never had a bad night hanging out with this man.

One of the most compassionate and charismatic people I've ever met, Michael is also a deep listener who loves humanity and adventure.

Each year, he packs up everything to join 70,000 other people in the Nevada desert to participate in the phenomenon known as Burning

Man. When Michael felt he had put on a few extra pounds, he didn't just get back into shape; he trained to run a 31-mile race in the desert and placed 10th his first time out.

Michael's big into music, travel, and partying with his friends—and still crushes it at work. He's the modern Renaissance man, and never compromises his fun or life for business pursuits. Michael, my friends, is an example of finding financial freedom, conquering time, and living the good life. He is a Legend if I've ever seen one. (Okay, maybe I have a slight man-crush on him!)

We can all learn from Michael's example. Ask yourself, if you could rate the level of fun in your life right now from one to ten, what would it be? What is one thing you'll do today, this week, or this month to truly live the good life? With a few practical tips on how to treat ourselves better, lighten up, and explore this beautiful planet, we can also be some of the most interesting and fun-loving people in the world. But first, let's look at the flip side.

"Ye who turns the lights off last, wins"... Right?

During my days of pursuing all things business and financial success, I refused to prioritize my fun, exercise and even worse, my sleep. It almost killed me! Believe it or not, "Ye who turns the lights off last, wins" used to be one of my war cries when I worked in the financial industry. Nobody's ever won with this strategy—ever!

I was constantly stressed, exhausted, and angry. My relationships, employees, clients, and ultimately, my reputation suffered by getting in those few extra hours each night to feel important, needed, and relevant. (I also believe certain segments of our society give us the ole "pat on the back" for working harder regardless of the costs to our health and families.)

I now know how we must prioritize creating boundaries with our jobs and practicing self-care to build and live Legendary lives. We need to work smarter, not harder. We must implement healthy habits, and as I've mentioned about a million times, *put our phones down and not over-schedule our lives.*

This, by the way, is coming from a guy who way over-scheduled himself this week while writing this book. Yep, I still have things to work through and am guilty as charged! #accountability

We also need to prioritize fun, truly experiencing the joys of life, and rest and relaxation. Go to a concert. Take a nap during the day. Learn how to surf. Heck, you can even toast it all with an ice-cold Dos Equis!

Another super interesting man in my life is Alvaro Arauz, who has been a major inspiration and example for me when it comes to living life to its fullest. Alvaro never misses an opportunity to sit courtside at his beloved Atlanta Hawks, travel to Italy to practice photography, give back to the community by sitting on non-profit boards, or attend an important family outing. Here's the kicker. He's absolutely crushing it professionally and is arguably the top law firm consultant in the country. By reverse engineering his personal and career goals together, Alvaro has intentionally designed his dream life. He's built his empire without compromising his ambition, family, or passions. Both Michael Liss and Alvaro Arauz are living proof that we can truly have it all in life!

If we want to build the life of our dreams like Alvaro and Michael, we must also prioritize treating our bodies like temples. By now, we know how much of a priority our physical health is. Study after study shows when we exercise and eat right, we not only look better, we live much longer and feel better both inside and out. We have more self-confidence, an increased sex drive, and stand prouder and taller in public.

We've talked about garbage in, garbage out. If we bought a $100,000 car, we wouldn't let it rust or fill it with soda instead of premium gas, right? So why would we plow through a bag of Doritos as a regular habit? I'm guilty as charged on overindulging once in a while—Krispy Kreme doughnuts and Ben & Jerry's Americone Dream are my jam!

However, I partake in these a whole lot less these days so I can be at my best to serve myself and others. I also prioritize working out, which brings us to the next topic.

Exercise

Many others have written amazing books on fitness, so I'll just share what's worked for me and my clients. I believe we need to exercise our bodies at least six days a week—not less than 20 minutes and not more than 60 minutes. While exercise is great, it can also become an addiction and an escape from reality, which is why I have set these rules for myself. Plus, I want us to prioritize and make time to exercise our hearts, minds, and souls just as much as our bodies, which very few people do.

I believe our physical, mental, and emotional health is one big stew. If you don't have each ingredient, it won't taste right. Therefore, we need to exercise all of these muscles.

Start small. If every January you decide you'll go to the gym every day for four hours, you'll throw in the towel after only a few days. But what if you just did a 10-minute walk once a day and then increase it to a 15-minute walk three weeks later? You would make progress each day and not lose momentum. As my trainer Julie Tuff, who's also one of my best friends, always says, "Just do *something*."

A perfect day for me includes reaching my goal of 12,000 steps, or 5.5 miles. A perfect week includes two days of cardio, two days of hot yoga, and two days of strength training. If I'm lucky, I'll work out with Julie or another buddy, which helps me stay accountable to my routine and have fun while doing it.

I also take it outdoors, starting with hiking. My coaches encourage me to get out and hike in the mountains at least twice a month for both physical and spiritual growth. I mix up my workout routines through paddle boarding, swimming, and all things water sports. I found that variety is the key to making exercise fun and keeping me engaged.

Others might have to stick with stringent routines. Pick what's best for you but again, "Just do *something*!"

Nutrition

For nutrition, my goal is to have at least 50% of my meals plant-based. I've failed at this recently, but it's a goal nonetheless. Also, as a rule, I've learned anything white (with the exception of cauliflower and a few other foods) is not so good for you. Neither is living on hot wings and beer, which I did for years until I realized I had gained 60 pounds since college.

Good hydration is essential. As part of my morning routine, I drink:

- One pint of water immediately after waking
- Two pints of warm lemon water before 8:00 A.M.
- One final pint of water mixed with organic apple cider vinegar before 9 A.M.

This may seem extreme, but I absolutely love the feeling of being hydrated and cleansed first thing in the morning. Recently, I have also started intermittent fasting with the goal of eating only between noon and 8:00 P.M. To help, I drink bullet-proof coffee from a recipe provided by my good friend Dr. Peter Boulden. I absolutely *love* the way it tastes, and coffee is by far my favorite part of my morning routine. Shoot us a message. We would be happy to share Doc Pete's recipe with you.

Alcohol

I love me a great glass of red wine, a local craft IPA, or fine scotch with a good friend.

However, to explore our current society's fascination with alcohol, I highly recommend the book *This Naked Mind* by Annie Grace. Annie explores the fact that we live in an alcohol-centric culture, "even deluding ourselves that drinking is a vital and healthy part of life." Even worse, not drinking has become taboo. How crazy is that? Is it because we want to feel better about *our* need to drink? Hmmmmm.

When we overindulge, however, we eat poorly, perform poorly at work, and often risk our important relationships. As someone whose healthy eating, exercising, and decision-making habits go down the toilet when I drink too much, I now limit my alcohol dramatically throughout the week. Also, each year, I make it a point to cleanse my body and examine my relationship with alcohol. My goal is to take at least two, 30-day complete sabbaticals from alcohol.

With the work I now do, I am reminded on a regular basis of how we, as ambitious people, often look for something to numb us when life becomes too hectic. And remember, my dear friends, society *encourages* drinking as a way to unwind after stressful days (hello, Happy Hour)—but often, the drinking just causes more stress, more drinking . . . and, well, we know the rest of this story.

Rest

Rest is essential for us to be at our best regardless of what some gurus say. It has become sexy to talk about how hard we work and how little we sleep, especially as entrepreneurs. If the trend continues, eventually we'll be reading books and social media posts telling us we must *never* sleep in order to be successful.

In all seriousness, we must honor and refuel our bodies and minds in the form of sleep and downtime in general. I have experienced firsthand the damage lack of rest and sleep does to our bodies, those we love, and ultimately our lives and careers. Working until we drop or burn out in the endless pursuit of becoming successful or until we get "there," wherever "there" is, is a zero-sum losers' game. If we are exhausted along the never-ending pursuit of more, we will never enjoy the process, our wins along the way, and more importantly our lives.

As for sleep, my body and mind require between seven to eight hours a night for me to perform optimally. I've never met anyone who could run full speed with less than six hours of sleep over an extended period of time. Anyone who says four hours of sleep is all they need is lying to themselves. Sooner rather than later, they will experience a major burnout or even worse, an early departure from life.

Lightening Up and Winding Down

Throughout this book, we've learned a lot of words to eliminate from our vocabulary. Here's one we need to ensure we bring back to the forefront: *Fun*. Woot, woot! Fun is an essential part of life, and to me, life would not be worth living without a lot of fun and laughter.

What helps us lighten up, laugh, and enjoy this beautiful life? For myself and other very ambitious people, I highly recommend scheduling uncompromisable "fun" time. It's critical to honor this time—no postponing, no canceling. It's also important for us to mix up our fun activities often so we don't become bored and fall right back into the trap of working more.

Heather and I make it a point to take time off for ourselves without compromise. We schedule dates for at least one night a week and day trips or getaways two weekends a month. Our inner circles and teammates hold us accountable to this. As a result, we have never been closer. We also find it very healthy to schedule downtime apart. Heather will go on yoga retreats or yearly girls' trips while I take frequent mancations or go hiking by myself. This strengthens our relationships and recharges our batteries.

If we don't schedule these on the calendar, they won't happen. Fun is *fun!* I recommend one day a week and two weekends a month for fun only—no working. Again, we must mix up our fun so it doesn't become mundane or feel like work. Do this with your family and significant others. Make it a game. Have others hold you accountable.

Travel

I encourage everyone I meet to travel abroad. Whether we're chained to work, freaked out by the news, or simply feeling massive inertia, so many people stay confined to the U.S., or even to their state and hometown. Travel, however, is our best teacher. We learn how others live their lives, sometimes better than ours. Traveling abroad also brings awareness of our freedoms or the many other benefits we might have taken for granted at home.

Travel brings us all closer together as humans and cultures. Every time I visit Europe, I appreciate the way meals are prepared and enjoyed slowly. On the flip side, I appreciate American plumbing more and more. For those who haven't been to Europe yet, you'll definitely see what I'm talking about!

I want to experience it all, from the history to the people to the culture. I want to taste, touch, and feel everything. I also make sure to see the beauty in everything and everyone. When we start to experience these new places for ourselves, we realize how what we've been told has tainted our views of the world.

A scene in the movie "Good Will Hunting" illustrates this point beautifully. Robin Williams as the counselor says to Matt Damon, the genius janitor, "If I asked you about art, you'd probably give me the skinny on every art book ever written. Michelangelo—you know a lot about him—life's work, political aspirations, sexual orientation, the whole works, right? But you can't tell me what it smells like in the Sistine Chapel. You never actually stood there and looked up at that beautiful ceiling."

Nature

Speaking of beautiful ceilings, there is no more beautiful ceiling than nature. Whether I am traveling or at home, I take the time to immerse myself in nature to find my soul and spirituality, be present, and think. When in nature, I completely remove myself from social media and my phone. Nature recharges my batteries, especially when I'm hiking in the mountains with my dogs, Hodges and Annie. From the sunshine and the rain, to the fresh air on our skin, nature helps us find a oneness with everything and everyone on Earth. There's a great reason many of us call the mountains, deserts, beaches, and nature in general "our spiritual places." We feel like we're at home and at complete peace when becoming one with nature.

This is because we *are* one with nature. It's in our DNA—we're physically and inherently drawn to natural places. Something in us says there's something bigger than us in these places; they're quiet, peaceful, and give us a good feeling of being closer to the source of all that is. For me, nature is my church and the closest we can get to God. If this sounds woo-woo, just think of the last time you sat around a campfire staring into its flames, or on a beach watching the waves, feeling at peace and saying nothing—it's because nature is the best kind of reality TV.

I am feeling oh so peaceful just writing this. Take a deep breath in and a deep breath out, my beautiful humans, and think about your favorite natural place. Ahh, doesn't that feel so much better?

See the Good in the World

When we explore our beautiful Earth, we can choose to see either the beauty and goodness of a place, or not. I've never been anywhere I didn't enjoy, because I intentionally search for the charm. Seeing the world through open-mindedness and a positive lens will directly affect our experience. No matter where we are in the world, the color of our skin, the language we speak, or the politics around us, all of us are the same—we all want to be seen, heard, and loved.

Here's to prioritizing rest, fun, and looking up to actually see this amazing planet through our own eyes.

LEGENDARY ACTIONS & REMINDERS

- Aim for at least 20 minutes but no more than 60 of exercise per day, six days per week. Working out doesn't just mean going crazy on the elliptical or deadlifting 400 lbs.—we can go hiking, paddle boarding, or whatever floats our boat.

- If your eating habits make you feel sluggish, change them. At a minimum, make 50% of your meals without white food or animals. Watch the weight fall off of you.

- Read *This Naked Mind* by Annie Grace, and decide how you'll take control of alcohol in your life.

- Where in the world do you want to travel? Choose one place. Renew your passport. Spend some downtime researching flights, hotels, cultural experiences, and restaurants. Close your computer. Have conversations with colleagues and friends who might have traveled to your dream destination. You're halfway there already.

- If you do nothing else in this area, schedule time for fun. Mix up the activities so it doesn't become mundane or feel like work. Do this with your family and significant others. Make it a game. Have others hold you accountable.

Chapter 11

Cultivating Unconditional Self-Love

"Head up. Shoulders back." I repeat: "Head up. Shoulders back."

You are worthy. You are enough. You are lovable. Now's the time for us to believe these words down to the depths of our souls. If I can believe this, anyone can!

Unconditional love for ourselves and others—wow—this is a tough one for a lot of us. I understand how hard it is just to invest in ourselves, much less truly love ourselves. Trust me, I get it. However, I've seen how powerful the above affirmations have benefited me and my clients 1,000X. Once such powerful words start making their way into our hearts, our lives and relationships will never be the same again.

This might sound a bit woo-woo, but the practices of gratitude, forgiveness, and affirmations are major components to building and living Legendary lives.

Let me be clear: Cultivating unconditional self-love is one of the most difficult teachings in this book to master—harder than building wealth, networking your way to Richard Branson, or running 31 miles through the desert. We're all our own worst critics. However, when we begin to do the hard work, open our minds, and take continued action on the tasks in this chapter, we will become the true masters of our hearts and minds.

No matter what happens to us during our time here on Earth, we're going to be okay. You know why? Because all of us are **worthy**, **enough,** **and lovable.** Let's learn how to truly believe this through practicing forgiveness, affirmations, and planning for our ideal future one year from now via an epic gratitude exercise of "thanking ourselves." (Wow, what a concept!)

When the Inner Critic Appears

It's important to note right from the beginning that unconditional self-love and respect can be difficult to achieve when our inner critic takes over. I call mine the "Tommy Go Round," which pays homage to one of my earliest mentors, Kerry Geho. I also know it's our biggest enemy. I'm many years into this work and consider myself a craftsman in all things self-development.

Still, as I write, I have fears and insecurities to overcome every day. However, I look forward to facing this battle now and have accepted the war to defeat the self-critic will never end until my last breath! Our self-critic only has one job, to make us suffer. This is why I do the hard work daily to build my mental, emotional, and spiritual fortress to aid in this never-ending fight.

Now let's learn the tools and strategies to silence our inner critic and cultivate unconditional self-love for ourselves and others.

Now is The Time

Growing up, and throughout my career in the financial world, I bottled up *everything*. I thought it was weak to show any type of emotion, fear, and especially need for help. However, after hundreds of conversations with other ambitious people, I now know I'm not alone in this. In the past, it was extremely difficult for me to show appreciation, love, and forgiveness to the people I cared for the most. This was because I struggled to appreciate, love, or forgive myself.

One of my biggest fears in life is dying with regrets. For all of us, it's time to seize this day and start living our lives. Right now is our chance to avoid regretting not taking that first step toward that big dream, saying what we need to say to someone we care about, and forgiving ourselves for a big mistake or someone who hurt us. Carpe diem, my dear friends!

Forgiving Ourselves and Others

We can boil forgiveness down to three steps:

1. Forgive ourselves.
2. Forgive others.
3. Let go and move on.

Let's expound on these.

Forgiving ourselves goes beyond looking in the mirror and saying, "I'm sorry" for the things we've done. We can take inventory of those we've hurt, accept 100% ownership for our mistakes, hold ourselves accountable, and finally ask the other person to forgive us. The regrets we hold on to and continuously beat ourselves up over are weighing us down.

Taking ownership and asking for someone to forgive us—in person—is powerful medicine. It's important to ask *all* the people we've wronged for forgiveness. If you cannot see them or they won't see you, send them a letter. Seeing them face to face is a powerful thing, though. You get to look them in the eye. If he or she is no longer alive, say a prayer or send a forgiving thought out to the universe.

Self-forgiveness took me a long time. I was hard on myself because I came from a life of bullying, violence, and abuse. I couldn't let go of what I experienced, and I became what I hated: the bully who harmed others. I felt unworthy of happiness and love.

The hardest part was realizing what those feelings were. It took time, therapists, mentors, coaches, good people around me, and affirmation practices. I had to exercise my love and forgiveness muscles often, and it was extremely challenging. (I still exercise these muscles *every day* and let me tell you, they are stronger than ever.)

My male mentor at the time, Kerry Geho, a longtime leader in a recovery program, guided me through this process. I took inventory of my wrongs and wrote the letters. I made a list of all I had done and reached out to as many people as possible. Many in person, some by letter, and some who were already gone. Writing everything down was refreshing, truly allowing me to move forward and stop regretting my past. If we never talk about these things or keep them bottled up, they eventually destroy us one way or another.

Be very careful choosing the person to walk with you in this process. Kerry didn't judge. When I shared terrible things I had done, he would say, "Oh, yeah! I've been there, too, my brother!" It helps us realize we aren't alone. People make mistakes. When we talk to a trusted mentor and bring the shadows out of the closet and state them out loud, it's very freeing. It doesn't mean we are unaccountable for our actions, but when we can see the why behind our past actions, we start the process of unconditional love for ourselves, and the healing begins! Kerry helped me understand I had been acting from a survival- and fear-based system—not Tommy Breedlove's value system.

Asking others for forgiveness was also a huge eye-opener for me. I would say nine out of ten people I approached didn't even remember what I did, thinking I was only reaching out to catch up. They took my apology respectfully and gratefully, but most told me I needed to let it go, which I did. This was powerful!

What holds us down is often in our heads. The point is to let it go and move forward instead of regretting the past. When I arrived at the end of the "people-I-hurt" list and had moved through the apologies, we burned that damn thing in Kerry's backyard. He jokes the fire is still burning today and always will be. I truly love and owe so much to that man!

The Birthplace of Forgiveness

If a person hurts us, 99 out of 100 times, he or she acted out of fear, insecurities, anger, or something instilled in them at a very young age. Sometimes even at an older age, it could be some sort of trauma, abuse, or neglect.

All of these wounds make us survivors and warriors. Unhealthy survival mechanisms can kick in when we want to be safe, seen, heard, and loved. If we can understand this and see the pain in ourselves and others—realizing they've been hurt in life, too—we can see ourselves in them. This place of empathy is the birthplace of forgiveness.

When we realize some of our past transgressions have helped us survive, we can actually *thank* ourselves for these mistakes. Some of my violence-based actions kept me alive in certain situations as a young man. When we see how behaviors and beliefs are no longer serving us and are now holding us back, it's powerful to give them a moment of gratitude for serving us—and then let them know we're moving on with our life without them.

Forgiving others means keeping them in our hearts and staying in a place of compassion and empathy. So many of our actions happen unconsciously from a place of fear, confusion, and ignorance. These emotions will eat us from the inside out and kill us if we hold on to them. Forgiving allows the healing process to begin now.

The Health Benefits of Forgiveness

Whether we choose to practice forgiveness or hold on to the anger and resentment, our physical and mental health are directly impacted. Johns Hopkins University Medical expert Karen Swartz shared that forgiveness can lower our risk of heart attacks, improve our cholesterol levels and quality of sleep (super important!), and reduce any pain, anxiety, depression, or other stress and health issues we experience in our lives. Chronic anger, on the other hand, puts us in a fight-or-flight mode, causing all kinds of negative health effects that can lead to fatal consequences.

Let Go of the Past

Failing to forgive ourselves and others keeps us stuck living in the past—and thus prone to giving up. This can also cause resentment, anger, and fear. The past, if we allow it, can constantly interrupt the present moment and become a self-given poison and prison. Also, if we don't forgive someone else for the harm they've done, we allow them to continue hurting us.

Holding on to the pain can cause us to miss out on a happy, fulfilled life of meaning. When we forgive, we release all of the bitter feelings we have about the past. Releasing the past allows us to enjoy the present. To fully live in the present and not worry about the future, we must also remember we all make mistakes and feel guilt.

Guilt is very different than shame, and it's critical for us to understand this. Guilt, as researcher and author Brené Brown explains, is when we have done something bad. Shame is believing we *are* bad. Shame is given to us by society, our parents, our politicians, and our religions and is completely false.

However, when we need to feel guilty for something we have done wrong, we need to own up to our actions without letting them define us or keep us from making our greatest impact. Whether I'm asking for forgiveness from myself or someone else, I'll say, "I did this. I regret doing it, and I'm sorry."

Forgiveness Takes Practice

Some of us have been through some terrible events—I've heard it all through my executive coaching, and nothing surprises me anymore. There really is no limit to what human beings can and will do to each other in certain situations, which can make forgiveness really tough. This means we might have to practice forgiveness many times before we really feel it in our hearts.

If we need to get in front of a mirror and scream, we can get in front of a mirror and scream. If we need to rage, we can rage. Just don't hurt anyone or yourself. Grab a pillow and allow yourself to feel the intensity. It's all part of the process. This will include feeling sadness and sorrow. Sometimes you just need a good cry. I'm a 6'2" 200 plus lb. alpha male, and sometimes a good cry is exactly what I need.

We must practice forgiveness daily at a minimum. The more we practice it (perhaps two or three times a day when we are truly hurting), the quicker we'll heal and be forgiven.

Affirmations

I get it. Forgiveness is hard, and it sucks sometimes. So here's an easier and more fun step toward cultivating unconditional self-love: affirmations. Every day, I say an affirmation by Gay Hendricks, which I learned from his epic book, *The Big Leap*.

"I expand in love, success, and abundance every day as I inspire others around me to do the same."

OMG, that is so profound and powerful! On a side note, I actually require my clients to read his book when we work together. I've never had a single person not be positively affected by *The Big Leap*.

If this reminds you of a certain fictional character on *Saturday Night Live* in the 1990s making fun of affirmations, well, so be it. Yes, it can feel silly or for us alphas, even weak. However, what's wrong with implementing something new into our strategy if what we are doing is not currently working?

If I go a day without writing my affirmations, I feel the negative effects. I'm just not the same. Every day, I write down my affirmations alongside my gratitude list, and remind myself to feel them as well. Here are some examples:

- I am worthy, enough, and lovable.
- I am so grateful that I see the love, learnings, and goodness in everything, everyone, and every situation.
- I am so thankful and happy that love, joy, goodness, money, wealth, and success flow easily, frequently, and abundantly to me.

Since implementing these affirmations into my daily routine, I've felt the profound effects on my mind and heart. I have actually rewired myself to be able to feel, give, and receive love. With affirmations, my happiness, self-respect, love for others, self-esteem, confidence, and success have increased 1000 times!

The Path to Peace

One day, during my sacred morning time, I came up with the following passage. I call it "The Path to Peace."

To truly find peace in our lives, we must let go of perfectionism, our expectations of others, and our need to believe we are in control. We can always influence, lead, teach, and guide, but we will never be in control. Our desire for perfection and control are illusions filled with ego and are truly unattainable. At the end of the day, nothing is in our control with the exception of our choices and mindset. Once we truly understand and accept this reality, peace and serenity will soon follow.

You can choose to use the above affirmations I've shared or create your own. When we say something enough, we truly start to believe it because (A) the affirmations are true, and (B) we're rewiring our brains and hearts from the shame of our past.

Planning for the Ideal Future

As we discussed earlier, gratitude is a huge part of mastering our mindsets and loving who we see in the mirror. Here's a truly Legendary tactic I learned recently. If you want to know what to focus on both personally and professionally, write yourself a thank you letter to be opened one year from now. Incorporate spiritual, emotional, mental, as well as your professional life and goals into it. This is thanking ourselves for living out our vision of what we want our lives to look like from A to Z.

I recently discovered this gratitude exercise from Shelton Davis with the Empathy Lab—thank you, my brother. You don't have to wait a year for the effects to kick in, either. I cannot wait to hear how your life improves by just doing this one Legendary action.

Do you believe you can truly have it all in life starting with unconditional love? I 100% do and hope you are starting to as well!

P.S. I love you, and especially you alphas!

LEGENDARY ACTIONS & REMINDERS

- Follow the three steps of forgiveness.
  o Forgive yourself.
  o Forgive others.
  o Let it go and move on.
- To begin forgiving yourself, take a personal inventory of those you have hurt, take 100% ownership in your mistakes, hold yourself accountable, and finally ask the other person to forgive

you. If you cannot ask the other person face-to-face, write a letter—even if they have passed away.

- Remember, we will never truly have rewarding relationships with friends and our romantic partners until we unconditionally love ourselves first.

- To begin forgiving others, remind yourself how survival mechanisms can kick in when we want to be safe, seen, heard, and loved. If we can understand this and see it in ourselves and others—realizing they've been hurt in life, too—we can see ourselves in them. This place of empathy is the birthplace of forgiveness.

- Remember to watch out for the negative self-talk or the inner critic saying we aren't good enough. Begin killing this SOB with all the tools in this book.

- Alongside your gratitude list, write the following affirmation out daily:
  - I am so grateful that I see the love, learnings, and goodness in everything, everyone, and every situation.
  - I am enough, worthy, and lovable.
  - I am so thankful and happy that love, joy, goodness, money, wealth, and success flow easily, frequently, and abundantly to me.
  - I expand in love, success, and abundance every day as I inspire others around me to do the same.

- Write yourself a thank-you letter for your successes and wonderful life one year from now.

- If you do nothing else, start forgiving yourself now for the mistakes of your past. Don't ever look into the rearview mirror because you're no longer going that direction. Carpe diem!

Chapter 12

Intimate Relationships with Others

When many people first meet my friend Tom Schwab, they're pretty amazed. Tom graduated from the U.S. Naval Academy in 1987 with a bachelor's degree in mechanical engineering. His first job after graduation was running a nuclear power plant, which he did for five years before spending twelve years in manufacturing, operations, and sales for a large medical device company, earning his MBA along the way.

Today, Tom is a podcast expert. He is now at the cutting edge of the marketing world, with a premier agency called Interview Valet that helps business owners, executives, and authors market themselves on other people's shows. How did he do it? There was no "podcast interview marketing" program or manual. It came down to relationships.

Tom spent years building relationships with business owners, executives, authors, and podcasters. He loved hanging out with growth-minded people looking to make a positive impact on their world. He loved marketing, positive messages, and business. These were *his* people, and he quickly built deep, intimate relationships with hundreds of people. (I was one of those people.)

Candidly, Tom is one of the most genuine, authentic people I've ever met. He is a straight shooter, *always* offering unfiltered advice whenever it's needed. He is wise beyond his years and a consistently attentive listener. With so many authentic relationships, Tom had little trouble finding podcasters willing to interview his clients, and also referrals to new clients and podcasters.

In a few short years, Tom has matched *hundreds* of clients with *thousands* of podcasts to reach *millions* of podcast listeners. Imagine the number of lives changed by those interviews—and all because Tom Schwab built intimate relationships with good people.

Building intimate relationships, however, does much more than boost our business. When we remove our masks and reveal our authentic selves, as we'll discuss in this chapter, we climb another Legendary step toward real happiness, lifelong fulfillment, and a new meaning of success.

Get Deeper

We've seen—not only through Tom's story, but also throughout this book—our need to become truly genuine, embrace transparency, and build authentic relationships with others. So, how do we accomplish this? It starts by committing to connecting with people on a deeper level at home and at work. We need to learn *who people are*, not *what they do*. We also need to focus on people's actions, not their titles, to understand where they best fit in our business and personal lives.

How do we feel when someone asks, "What do you do?" We've been unconsciously wired to ask this question whenever we meet someone new. However, it's a size-up question for us to see if we're ahead of or behind them in the game of life. It's also fishing to see if they can somehow help us. Nothing more, nothing less. Just to add on a bit more, asking someone "what they do," is the first move of an amateur and not a pro!

Better questions might be: "What is something interesting you're working on?" or "What are you learning?" Authentic relationships come from cutting out the materialistic B.S. and connecting on a different level. I seek to discover if our values are in line with each other and if we enjoy the same things. When we meet someone new, getting deeper quicker is the best way to discover if this person is a fit for our tribe.

Our Masks

During the journey of becoming authentic, we need to stop and take a good hard look in the mirror to see what we are pretending in public to be. For some reason, we all wear masks to fit in or feel important because we care so much about what other people think. It's as if we're afraid to be who we truly are out of fear that others will not like us or accept us.

All of us desire to be seen, loved, heard, and accepted. We all want to feel like a member of a tribe. We all want to feel important and therefore we put on fake masks to fit in.

Here are some masks:
- I'm funny.
- I'm important.
- I'm the life of the party.
- I'm tough.
- I'm sexy.
- I'm powerful.
- I'm stoic and never need to ask for help!
- I'm a hard worker.
- I'm always right.
- I'm a bully.
- I'm a victim.
- I'm a name-dropper (ugh—this one makes my skin crawl.)

The truth is, all of these masks scream: "I don't think I'm enough! I'm scared and insecure and need you to *love* me—*please!*" Here's the kicker: we all have worn at least two masks during our lives, and most of us are still suffering from the need to hide behind one or multiple of these ego-filled, superficial masks. It's about time we admit to ourselves when we're pretending to be someone other than who we are.

Let me be clear. I am right there with you fine people. I have worn *so* many masks over my life, especially during my professional career in the accounting and financial consulting world. I felt I needed to be the party guy, funny guy, sexy guy, never-ask-for-help guy, and, finally, "Ye who turns the lights off last wins" ("I'm the hardest worker") guy. None of those masks were actually me. To riff on Eminem, "Would the real Tommy Breedlove please stand up?"

"To be yourself in a world that is constantly trying to make you something else is the greatest accomplishment."
–Ralph Waldo Emerson

I thought I never wore the stoic mask. How wrong I was on that front. The stoic mask is the guy who will not ask for help or show weakness. I have now gone from never asking for help and never saying "I don't know" to always asking for help and being okay with not knowing everything—which allows me to be me.

Now I wear only one mask: the Tommy Breedlove mask (which isn't really a mask at all, because I am just myself). However, I must confess there are still days I battle to *not* put on certain masks and say things I don't believe just to fit in. I believe this will always be a war for all of us (worthy of fighting, I must add). However, I do the hard work every day in my morning routine to become the master over my thoughts and to cultivate unconditional love for myself so that I know the real me is enough.

I really wish I had figured all of this out before I almost destroyed myself, my career, and those I cared about. You know what, though? I would not be the man I am today without all of the scars, triumphs, and tragedies. I now embrace and am thankful for mistakes and my past. I stand on them as a base to be better today than I was yesterday.

I believe we will never be truly happy, fulfilled, and peaceful until we embrace the person we really are and were born to be.

Once we embrace who we truly are, we naturally remove the masks and throw them into the garbage. Then, we can build our own tribe of people we want to travel with us on this journey we call life. We're not going to make everyone happy, just as we're not going to make everyone sad. Every day, we work to become immune to what others think and say. We strive to be our authentic selves. Eventually, we develop the mantra, "What other people think of me is none of my business!"

Authenticity

Unconditional self-love, which we discussed in Chapter 11, promotes authenticity, fulfillment, and success in all facets of our lives. In order to be authentic, we must look in the mirror and be honest with ourselves and know we are not perfect. We all have great strengths as well as blind spots and weaknesses. As the great spiritual traditions state: Know thyself!

When we truly accept and embrace who we are, we don't have to *fake* anything. This leaves us feeling at peace, and with more courage and more time for the important work. For these reasons, it's important to not only pursue authenticity but also to avoid making time for people who are inauthentic.

We must understand, own, and honestly communicate our strengths and weaknesses to our families and our work and life communities. When we're vulnerable and speak honestly and openly about ourselves, it gives permission for others to do the same. We give others the gift of going second when we courageously break the honesty and vulnerability ground first.

When I'm coaching someone on business and am raw and honest about my mistakes and the learnings from them, I can see the client visibly relax. All of a sudden, they're ready to share their fears and vulnerabilities—a huge step in authenticity, trust, and relationship-building. This is a great example of me giving my client "the gift of going second."

Authenticity and vulnerability are also key to being a great leader at home and at work. Demonstrating them inspires trust and encourages others to step up and aid us in pursuing greater success and happiness.

Important: If you want to take your relationships to a whole new level, be vulnerable with your significant other. Tell him or her a major fear of yours. Or even better, reveal your deepest, darkest secret and why you were scared to share it. If they truly love you, this will make them love you even more. When both partners are vulnerable, we feel a thousand times closer to each other along with the incredible feeling of a giant weight lifted off our shoulders.

According to a recent University of Pennsylvania research project undertaken by Abigail a, being our authentic self has a positive correlation to our well-being *even when doing so sets us apart from others.*[4] This research shows humans have a need to be unique. *Yes!* The project also correlates authenticity with higher levels of overall life satisfaction and well-being. I know for a fact I have personally felt higher levels of peace and well-being by just being me!

---

4   Mengers, Abigail. (2014). The Benefits of Being Yourself: An Examination of Authenticity, Uniqueness, and Well-Being.

Listen to Oscar Wilde: "Be yourself; everyone else is already taken."

Here are a few more authenticity reminders:
- Always be you, and use your real voice. Your tribe will love it! What sounds ordinary to you is extraordinary to others.
- The things that make you weird as a kid are what make you great today. Accept this, and believe in your gifts.
- Our biggest fear is being seen as we really are. However, our most important job is to fall in love with our authentic selves in order to be able to truly build intimate relationships with others.

No matter who comes into our lives, we must develop a clear vision of and commitment to the life and legacy we want to build for ourselves and others. Instead of worrying about what other people think, we must surround ourselves with people who align with our passions, purpose, and value systems.

We've got important things to do and places to go. We do not have time for fake or inauthentic people who are emotionally draining. Removing the masks and the fake people from our lives is so beautifully freeing.

Relationships at Home

I often ask the question, "Am I the same person at home when nobody is watching compared to the person I am in public?" This is one of the biggest mistakes we make as humans. Time and time again, we treat our colleagues like royalty. Then, when the doors close behind us at home, we treat our family like garbage. It's a sad fact but true.

For some reason, we believe our loved ones are convenient and often take them for granted. We think we'll get back to them someday once we "get there" or have conquered our next conquest. It's an epidemic, my beautiful humans, and I hear it quite often in my relationship and mindset coaching. I believe this has become such an issue that I include the question on my weekly accountability check-in with my clients.

"The definition of a good marriage is a contest of generosity."
—David Whyte

I also ask my inner circle to hold me accountable to this core value. Just the other day, I caught myself continuing to work and write this book when my beautiful wife came home. I let myself keep working without telling her I love her, kissing her, or asking her how her day was. What a giant mistake. She's the most important person in my life and is always there for me unconditionally. So why did I not choose her first over my work? Ugh. I am still working on being the best me, my wonderful humans! #accountability

Ask yourself how you speak to your significant other, children, or parents. What would happen if you treated your business peers, or friends the same? Don't you think we owe it to ourselves and the people we care about the most to be the same person behind closed doors as we are in public?

Our Three Marriages

Do you believe you're in three marriages? I now do.

The great Irish poet, David Whyte, teaches that the sooner we honor the following three marriages, we'll all be happier, more fulfilled, and more successful as a couple.

Each of us is married to:

- our spouse
- our work/purpose
- and ourselves

When I stepped back and meditated on this, I 100% agree.

Here's to honoring our three marriages!

Listening Deeply

One of our problems, especially in business—is when people are talking, we're thinking of the next thing to say as opposed to truly listening to them. In order to create and foster the best relationships, we need to truly listen to our fellow humans and be fully present in the conversation. When we do this, our response will be pure because it'll be related to what they actually said and not what we think we heard. By the way, our clients, friends, and, most importantly, our romantic partners crave us to truly hear them. I repeat: *They love it when we truly hear their point of view.*

This is also the best way to cultivate trust and loyalty. I'll say this is again as it's Super Important: Deep listening is the best way to cultivate trust and loyalty. Listening deeply and presently can have a massively positive impact on our lives and relationships.

As the author of *The 12 Rules for Life* Jordan Peterson puts it, "We must realize the person we're speaking to probably knows something we don't, regardless of their stage in life." Epic book, by the way, and a must-read! Jordan writes, "We must put aside our autobiographies and points of view when listening, and then listen twice as much as we speak."

Think about it. There's a reason that we have two ears and one mouth. If you want to be a great salesperson or 10X your income, it all starts with deep listening! When we do this, we will hear their emotions and feelings—always seeking to understand—with empathy and compassion. We must also remember how sometimes saying nothing is better than saying anything.

Deep listening and meaningful conversations lead not only to better relationships but more happiness. A study by psychologist Matthias Mehl found happy people spend 66% of their conversations speaking about substantive topics (where meaningful information is exchanged) and only 33% on small talk.[5] "How about the weather?" and "Did you see the game on TV last night?" Sure, these can be ice-breakers sometimes, but we must use our listening skills to advance to a deeper level of conversation if we want to build solid relationships and find more happiness.

Certainty: the Killer of all Things Trust and Intimacy

Anytime we become certain of one philosophy, way of thinking, or idea and lose our ability to listen to others and see their point of view, disaster strikes. Certainty leads to breakups in relationships, divorce,

---

5   Mehl, Matthias R., Simine Vazire, Shannon E. Holleran, and C. Shelby Clark. "Eavesdropping on Happiness." *Psychological Science* 21, no. 4 (2010): 539–41. https://doi.org/10.1177/0956797610362675.

war, or stagnation to growth. A great example is Galileo, who was almost burned alive for saying the Sun, and not the Earth, was the center of our solar system.

Here's another, modern-day example. In my former business career, one of my partners believed the customer was always right. They were so afraid of saying no, renegotiating the price, or telling them they were incorrect at any cost. Their certainty to the customer is always right almost cost our firm everything. As financial auditors, our job was to a.) give the client advice, b.) tell them when they were incorrect, and c.) (most importantly), tell the outside world—i.e. the stock market, banks, investors, etc.—that our clients were doing the right thing and their numbers were correct enough to be safely relied upon.

Because of the inability to say no nor take the advice from the other partners, this person decided to keep a client we knew was dishonest and a bad fit for our firm. As a result, we were named as the defendant in a mega multimillion-dollar lawsuit. We lost two employees, our reputation, and a very trusted referral source because of my partner's need to be certain. This is a prime example of a major loss happening because of someone's certainty and being unwilling to change their mindset.

Keeping an Open Mind

The older I get and the more I read, learn, and travel, the more I realize I know nothing. I was taught at a very young age to fear and distrust certain people and places. However, the more I travel and read, the more I realize that all humans want to be safe, seen, heard, and loved.

It's really that freaking simple. When we become certain about anything, we lose the ability to form truly intimate and authentic relationships with our fellow humans. I now stop, pause, and think when I hear statements like, "One man's terrorist is another man's freedom fighter." Hmm.

We can be confident in what we believe while still keeping our minds open and compassionate to the opinions of others. I believe it's important to welcome other viewpoints, even those questioning our beliefs. If a new lesson calls our beliefs into doubt, let's take them into consideration.

It's natural to feel as if we know what's right and believe things won't change, yet history has proven even our most certain beliefs to be untrue many times. One great example was the belief that the Earth was flat. Many people wanted to put scientists to death in horrible ways just for saying the planet was round. In extreme cases, we've killed each other and gone to war because we became so sure of one belief versus another.

Whether on a small or large scale, certainty leads to us believing there is only one choice. Over time, this leads to close-mindedness, which results in loss of love, compassion, and respect for the opinions of others. Thus, it kills intimacy and trust forever.

Judgment, Mirrors, and Seeing the Best in Others

It's human nature to judge others, especially when we're assessing potential new relationships. A Buddhist friend reminded me one day that when I judge others, I'm actually looking into the mirror of my own soul and seeing the things I don't like about myself. Now that's powerful stuff, my friends!

When someone else's actions irritate us, we can ask: "Am I doing the same thing without being aware of it? Can I look inside myself first before criticizing them to make sure I'm not acting in a slightly different way?" If we have the good sense to do this each time we're shocked by someone else's actions, we'll realize our relationships with others are like mirrors presenting to us the things we need to work on in our own lives.

If we don't see this, we're deluding ourselves. We might think our behavior is inoffensive, but it becomes monstrous as soon as we see it in others. Learning to be aware of our judging brings compassion to ourselves, our relationships, and the people around us.

Nearly everything irritating us is a lesson. It's an opportunity to practice open-mindedness and see where others are coming from or maybe even ask what's going on in their lives so we can help. If someone cuts us off in traffic, we don't know if they are sick, making their way to a dying kid, or just being a complete ass. We truly don't know.

When I experience bullying, I recognize it in myself from my former life and have an urge to want to become a bigger bully. My deepest darkest desire is to show them they can't bully or continue to hurt me or others. Instead of lowering myself to their standards, I now practice pausing, letting my anger go, and then setting forceful, compassionate boundaries with the person bullying me. It's also a great time for me to practice empathy to ideally see their point of view or what's going on in their lives. Deep down inside, 99 out of 100 people are wonderful humans and are acting out of their value systems when they are hurting others.

Becoming angry and judgmental instead of reflecting is a complete waste of time and energy. Yet we expect perfection in others when we're not even close to realizing it in ourselves. Gentle reminder: There's no such thing as perfection. Perhaps if we started seeing the best in people and not looking for the worst, we'd discover more peace in our own lives.

"To love is to recognize ourselves in another."
—Eckhart Tolle

...And a Few Words on Gossip

We now know how to nurture intimate and trustful relationships with colleagues, friends, clients, and significant others. The surest way to kill these relationships, however, is to gossip. If someone talks poorly about another person, they'll surely talk about us the same way to others.

Most positive people, including yours truly, despise gossiping! Let's commit to not talking about our fellow humans in a negative way, period. Instead, let's use the many tools in our Legendary toolbox for building and maintaining intimate relationships and to live a judgment-free authentic life.

As a final friendly reminder, building and maintaining intimate relationships with others has some major benefits:

- People trust us.
- We gain courage.
- Our income increases due to our authenticity.
- Our success in life and business increase as people want to help us.
- And the best of all, our sex lives dramatically improve. BOOM!

These are all giant "Hell Yeses" for me! Here's to building intimate and authentic relationships, my fellow beautiful humans!

LEGENDARY ACTIONS & REMINDERS

- Instead of asking new acquaintances "What do you do?" ask them, "What is something interesting you are working on?" or "What are you currently learning?"
- Repeat after me: "What other people think of us is none of our business!"
- Give others the gift of going second by courageously being vulnerable first.
- Always be you, and use your real voice. Your tribe will love it!

- Things that make you weird as a kid are what make you great today. Accept this, and believe in your gifts.

- Our biggest fear is being seen as we really are—but our most important job is to be and fall in love with ourselves in order to build intimate relationships.

- Be vulnerable with your significant other. Tell him or her a major fear of yours. Or even better, reveal your deepest darkest secret and why you were scared to share it. If they are in a good place and truly love you, this will make them love you even more. Show vulnerability, and you will feel a thousand times closer to them along with a giant weight lifted off your shoulders.

- Do you talk about people's weaknesses, mistakes, or issues when they are not there? If so, why? This is gossip and tells others we will do the same to them. Serve yourself and others by killing gossip.

- If you do nothing else, regularly ask yourself the question, "Am I the same person when nobody is watching or behind closed doors as I am in public?"

ULTIMATE LEGENDARY CHALLENGE

Are you truly certain about anything? If so, research and explore the people with differing opinions. Do you see any truth in their belief? Do you see where they are coming from without judgment? Would you be willing to have a conversation to help build empathy and open-mindedness? (See MLK, Gandhi, Mother Teresa, Jesus, Buddha for inspiration.)

Chapter 13

The Power of Choice

In *Man's Search for Meaning*, Viktor Frankl recounts the three years he spent in Nazi concentration camps. Frankl lost his parents, brother, and wife to the Nazis and witnessed the worst horrors imaginable. His reflections and observations give us a rare glimpse into the mind of a true Legend and reminds us of the biggest power we possess: choice.

To demonstrate the power of choice, Frankl recounts two groups of concentration camp prisoners. The first group chose to help the Nazis operate the concentration camps. Some held formal positions and helped maintain order within the camp. Others turned in their fellow prisoners for violating rules knowing the Nazis would torture or even kill them. They made these choices in hopes of earning better treatment and avoiding their own suffering. As Frankl describes it, this group turned against their own people and personal value systems; they gave up on love and compassion; they chose survival over integrity.

The second group of prisoners made different choices. They refused to help the Nazis even though they knew they would be tortured and killed. They chose pain and death over turning against their own people, sacrificing their value systems, and contributing to the horror. These

Legendary humans may have paid the ultimate price, but did so with dignity and their core values intact.

Everyone has the freedom to choose—even in severe suffering. This is, in my humble opinion, one of the biggest lessons for us to remember when building and living Legendary lives. We can choose to participate in our own rescue. We can choose goodness, greatness, and truth. We can choose to kill blame—and we can choose to do the one thing to make our lives 100 times better.

Everything is a Choice

The power of choice is truly the one thing we actually control in our lives. Everything else is 100% not in our power to control. Each and every day, each and every moment we spend with someone or on something, the decisions we make are completely in our power. How wonderful is that realization?

Everything, and I mean absolutely everything, is a choice:

- Our mindsets
- Our attitudes
- Whether we see the good or bad in the world
- How we react to situations
- Where we spend our precious time
- What we believe in
- The people we surround ourselves with

In certain situations, we believe we only have one choice. The truth is we always have more than one choice. If we examine the situations when we believe we are without choice, we don't actually find an *absence of choice*. Most of the time, we just cannot find a *choice we like*. We must choose between two or more bad choices. Unfortunately, sometimes we have to make a seemingly bad choice for the right reasons. However, there is always a choice.

Throughout this chapter, we'll take a deep dive into our power of choice. As we truly embrace this, we discover goodness, aspire for significance and greatness, and see giving in an all new light.

Choosing to Participate in Our Own Rescue

Sometimes the most profound wisdom comes from the most unusual places. This nugget was given to me by a river rafting guide in preparation for a trip down the Gauley River. For reference, the Gauley is a beast of a river and has multiple Class V-plus rapids, which is river speak for extremely dangerous. Prior to pushing off on our journey, the guide said to us: "You must participate in your own rescue."

To translate, he was helping us realize that ultimately our safety is in our own hands. If we were tossed out of the raft, we would have to choose to participate in our own rescue: turn over on our backs, keep our head and feet out of the water, look for a rope, and swim to safety. The alternative: death by drowning.

I had an epic "aha" moment, realizing this profound wisdom is completely relevant to life. There is no magic pill or hero coming on a white horse to save us. It's up to us to invest in ourselves and do the hard work to find happiness, success, and true meaning to life. No one can save us but us!

If we feel unfulfilled, unhappy, or find ourselves constantly in a state of anger, envy, or judgment, we can choose to *participate* and do something about it. If we wait until it's too late, we'll look back on our lives with regrets and should-haves.

So how do we do it? It's simple: make the best choices within our power. We choose to invest in ourselves first and make our emotional, mental, and physical well-being our full-time job. If this sounds selfish, it's actually not. It is the exact opposite. We must invest and serve ourselves first so we may invest and serve others better.

As we discussed in Chapter 11, investing in and loving ourselves first allows us to fully show up for our communities, family, friends, and businesses, and is one of the most important choices we can make. For some reason, we've been taught it's okay to put ourselves last. Nope! This makes us martyrs and, for most of us, causes resentment with the life we are living.

Isn't it interesting how we'll invest in the stock market, our career, people we don't know, and our family and friends prior to investing in ourselves? As a result of not prioritizing ourselves, we crumble quickly at the first sign of trouble or tragedy because we're not standing on a solid foundation.

Therefore, let's choose to participate in our own rescues and invest in ourselves first. Let's choose to be who we needed when we were younger so we can be such a person for the world today, leaving our mark on the world one amazing human at a time.

Choosing Goodness to Leave a Lasting Legacy

Aaron Walker is a man from humble beginnings who is well on his way to achieving Legendary status. Heck, he might already be there. He's touched hundreds of men's lives, especially mine. A very successful entrepreneur who's started and sold countless businesses, he now owns and operates the worldwide and incredibly powerful "Iron Sharpens Iron" mastermind group.

Aaron's following in the footsteps of his father by becoming a force for goodness. His father, Johnny, was a Legendary individual who, in Aaron's words, was just an ordinary man. Legends aren't always famous or wealthy. In fact, I would argue we've never heard of most Legends due to their modesty and grace.

Johnny was a carpenter who struggled to succeed in business throughout his life but was a born leader and learned to flourish by choosing goodness—the first to serve in times of need and show up for others. Very few people in the world know of Johnny but, in his Tennessee community, he's remembered as a Legend.

When Johnny passed away, Aaron was blown away by what he witnessed. People stood in long lines to offer condolences to him. Person after person told Aaron how Johnny had helped them during his life. Aaron and his siblings spent six hours listening to others' recollections of how Johnny had encouraged them, helped them, and impacted their lives. Seeing the legacy Johnny had left inspired Aaron, putting him on the path to living a Legendary life.

People who aspire to lead a life of significance strive to be a force for goodness for themselves, their families, and the communities they serve. Their objective is to put good in the world, leave an impact, and create a lasting legacy larger than themselves.

In *View from the Top*, Aaron discusses his choice of goodness: "The more time we spend endorsing, connecting, helping, and aiding others, the more we have a giving spirit." He writes, "The sooner we can genuinely develop this type of passion for those around us, the better. This mindset crosses all borders—whether in business or your personal life. When it's the end of my final day and they put me down six feet under, I want people to say, 'That man left a legacy of wisdom. He really searched God's heart. He lived a life that was true to himself and true to others.'"

Aaron doesn't just talk about bringing impact to the world; he follows through with his actions. This is yet another reminder of how it all begins with taking action. He urges us to: "Start giving today, incrementally. Donate an hour or two to the local nursing home. Buy a few meals for others anonymously. Bring an enormous smile to onlookers. Do a few random acts of kindness."

As we can learn from Aaron and Johnny, building a Legendary life starts with choosing goodness. Goodness is your character—who you truly are, a feeling you leave in yourself and others, and a way of being.

Choosing Goodness Always Leads to Greatness

Several years ago, I founded a movement called Choose Goodness. People have asked me, "Why don't you say, 'Choose Greatness?'" Well, greatness is a subjective measurement. Goodness is the feeling which comes from a deep, deep level inside of us. Some would call it our soul, heart, or love. This is the birthplace of compassion and authenticity.

Choosing Truth

"Sometimes, it's hard to admit the truth when we're scared of harming others or saying no. However, one way we can start honoring our word today is by simply showing up for ourselves (*with unconditional self-love*) and others (*with our complete attention and presence*) when we say we will and honoring our commitments. Just making this one simple promise will put us in the top 90% of all humanity."

Goodness is unconditional self-love and self-belief—lightening up on ourselves. My personal definition of goodness is having love, trust, and respect from those closest to me. This begins with me, my wife, Heather, my hounds, Hodges and Annie, and continues on to my friends, and finally to my business network. It starts and ends with serving and giving from our hearts authentically, without regard to others' opinions, expectations, or keeping score.

Goodness never hurts and is always altruistic, lifting ourselves and others up. A study by Yona Kifer of Tel Aviv University shares how altruistic emotions, actions, and behaviors bring us greater well-being, health, and life longevity.[6]

We can use our values as a compass to make our own rules rather than getting caught up in all the things we "should" do. I do believe, however, we can have it all—joy *without* compromising our ambition or business success.

Choose One Small Act a Day

Imagine how our world would be if we all chose to perform one act of kindness a day—sharing a word of encouragement, smile, or gift. These acts can be very simple and have an exponential effect on the world.

As most of us have heard about the "pay-it-forward effect," when we give acts of kindness, the receiver of the goodness then does the same for others (i.e. pays it forward). I'm a firm believer that everything we give, without expectation of receiving anything in return, comes back to us tenfold.

This point is illustrated so brilliantly in the lyrics to "People are Crazy" by Billy Currington. This great country song is about a man who meets an older gentleman in a bar, and they have an amazing conversation about love, life, tragedies, and triumphs.

Later in life, the younger man picks up a newspaper to see the old man, a millionaire, has passed away. The funny thing is, the old man left his fortune to some guy he barely knew. As the song goes, the old man's kids are mad as hell, but the young man, he's doing quite well. As a thank you, the younger man stops by the cemetery to say thanks, pray, and leave a six-pack of beer by the old man's gravestone. This beautiful and

6   Kifer, Yona & Heller, Daniel & Perunovic, Wei & Galinsky, Adam. (2013). The Good Life of the Powerful: The Experience of Power and Authenticity Enhances Subjective Well-Being. Psychological science. 24. 10.1177/0956797612450891.

inspirational song sums it all up. It's clear the younger man's authentic act of kindness and deep listening had an immense impact on the older man. Not crazy at all, really.

Who knows, one conversation of compassion might make us millionaires as well!

Choose to Kill Blame

Part of the power of choice is learning to take responsibility for our choices. The only person we have to blame for our situations is ourselves. The more we hold ourselves accountable for our choices, the more success we achieve and, ultimately, the better choices we make.

The more businesses that accept responsibility for their actions, the more customers and partners trust them and, ultimately, the more profits rise as a result. We will never become successful in business or life when we blame others or see ourselves as victims.

We are not only responsible for the negative consequences of our choices, but we also control our own happiness. If we want to feel happy, we must *choose* to be happy and not blame anyone else for the way we feel.

Blaming others for our failures and mistakes minimizes our roles in the choices as well as causes us to miss out on the beautiful learnings from the mistakes. Right now, our news and social media are always looking for someone else to blame. This behavior is causing us to become a victim society.

It's important to hold ourselves accountable and not blame others. Everyone messes up. We all fail. If we were perfect or immortal, life would be really boring. In that sense, maybe failure is the spice of life, and the choices we make in responding to failure are what make us either like a phoenix who rises from the ashes or an anchor holding us down.

The choice is ours. We can blame our parents, society, others, or the government for our problems, or we can commit to writing the rest of our story by taking back the power of our own choices.

Choose to See the Learnings

"Don't waste the hurt." Wow! An inspiring young man, Corey Hackett, said this while fitting me for a tuxedo. Talk about the power of choice and learning to see the goodness and learnings in the failures and pain. Pain is always temporary, but the lessons from it are forever. Shout out to Corey Hackett and Stephen Churn with Blank Label for the amazing conversations and making me look good at events and speeches.

Choosing the *One Thing*

Here's an incredible choice and challenge. Say to yourself: If I choose to do this *one thing*, or choose to stop doing this o*ne thing*, right now, it would benefit my life 100%.

I bet you knew immediately what your one thing is. I did! And here's the final kicker to this challenge:

Why are you not doing—or why are you still doing— this *one thing*?

The answer to this question is where your deepest insecurities lie. Now let's choose to lean into our lives and take action on our *one thing*!

P.S. Put the one thing in a safe place where you'll see it every day. Give it attention, intention, and love!

A final moment of gratitude. The above was my biggest takeaway from *The One Thing* written by Gary W. Keller and Jay Papasan. I want to send a special thank you to these fine gentlemen as this was an epic and life-changing read!

As a final reminder: love or hate, fear or abundance, happiness or sadness—these are all a choice, my beautiful humans!

LEGENDARY ACTIONS & REMINDERS

- Remember—we must choose to invest in our physical, mental, emotional, and spiritual health *first* by using the tools outlined in the book. When we invest in ourselves first, we are able to serve others and our businesses better.
- Stop blaming others. Know you are 100% responsible for your situation, choices, and mindset.
- Choose to perform one small act of kindness for yourself every day. Trust me, you deserve it.
- Choose to perform one small act of kindness for someone else every day. The key is to not keep score and expect nothing in return.
- If you do nothing else, ask yourself: What is the *one thing* I can start or stop doing, right now, that would benefit my life 100%? Why are you not making this choice?

Chapter 14

Never Giving Up

"On the plains of hesitation lie the blackened bones of countless millions, who at the dawn of victory, lay down to rest, and in resting died."

—Adlai Stevenson

Plagued by fear and hesitation for the first 36 years of life, that quote hits really close to home for me. I now know that life, success, and happiness are all about movement. Inertia equals certain death to all things progress.

Success in life and business is the direct result of:

- Feeling the fear and doing it anyway
- Continuing to take action
- Never giving up
- Finishing

Don't Stop—Don't *Ever* Stop

As we've discussed at length, success will never happen without taking action. However, *continued* action and never giving up, especially through the hardships, failures, and mistakes are where legends are truly born.

Becoming Legendary in work, love, and life is the result of sustained action. We are the creators of our own luck, greatness, and destinies—these are not simply handed to us. If we follow the legends who came before us—whether it's Martin Luther King, Alexander Hamilton, or Brené Brown, they do everything with intention, purpose, and passion. Just as important, they've all achieved greatness by refusing to give up when failures or challenges arose. JK Rowling, author of *Harry Potter,* and John Grisham, author of *The Firm,* had their work rejected countless times.

They simply didn't give up, are extremely successful, and make massive impacts!

Throughout this book, we discuss other aspiring Legends—regular folks just like you and me. People like those whose stories we've shared in this book. These are all ordinary people who have become extraordinary by discovering their purpose, choosing goodness, and never giving up. If they can do this, so can we!

Continue Showing Up

I believe simply showing up for ourselves, others, and especially our work is what puts us in the top 10% of all humans. The takeaway: show up every day, put in the time, and do the work. We will take action, fail, keep taking action, and fail again, time and time *again.*

A reporter once asked the great musician Dave Grohl, the former drummer for Nirvana and one of the founders of Foo Fighters, "How do we become a famous rock star just like you?" Dave told the guy to grab an old musical instrument from a yard sale, go down to your basement, invite your friends, and just suck. Keep grinding and continue to suck and continue to suck, and all of a sudden after all of that sucking, you become Nirvana.

This is a great example of what happens when we keep grinding away.

Isn't it amazing how every "overnight success" actually put in numerous years of hard work (that most of us never see), and they never gave up on their dreams? Nirvana didn't just start. They continued to take action, never gave up, and eventually became one of the most influential bands in the world.

In order for us to build and live Legendary lives, we must do the same, continuously working the tools in this book. Start *small*. Choose one thing, and continuously practice it until you start seeing results. Be patient, however, as nothing worth having in life comes easily!

The Enemy

Please open your minds and hearts to me for just a brief moment. It's time for a quick dive into the mystical world.

Without exception, when we begin doing the hard work and investing in our mental, emotional, and spiritual muscles, the damn Enemy shows up—100% of the time!

Some great spiritual teachings call the enemy demons, ego, or the yang to the yin. Others call it the dark side, evil, or the devil himself. I simply call it the Enemy. The Enemy literally has one job: to destroy our happiness, families, and lives. It's the evil force that wants to take down our newfound self-respect and confidence.

When we step in and step up to be the best versions of ourselves, we see the Enemy work overtime to keep us where we are: scared and stuck. Even worse, it wants us to fail and fall hard and fast. The Enemy would love nothing more than for us to self-sabotage and lose it all—including our lives.

This enemy comes in many forms. It's the voice in our heads that says we're not good enough and asks, "What if they find out our deepest, darkest secrets?" It's the major home repairs that occur right after you begin gaining control of your finances. The layoff when we've just moved into our new home. It's the shaming phone call from a relative after we've made a breakthrough in our marriage counseling. The list is endless.

It's not *if* the evil bastard will show itself, it's *when*!

I have great news, however. We can use massive weapons in the fight against this darkness. First, when the Enemy gets loud or a major setback occurs, we must double and sometimes triple down on our daily routines of self-development, especially around our mental and emotional fortresses. Practicing what we've learned in this book with more frequency is our best weapon in this fight.

This is why my trusted group of advisors holds me accountable for my daily meditation, gratitude, reading, and exercise practices. When we continuously take action on being mentally and emotionally stronger each and every day, as well as lean into our inner circle, we're better prepared to handle the difficult situations and self-sabotaging thoughts when they arise.

I used to believe this stuff was hocus pocus and fairy tales until I saw it time and time again in my coaching work and within my own life. Trust me, my fellow Legends in the making, this Enemy is very real and powerful. We will leave whatever *it* is up to the great spiritual teachers. However, we now have identified it and know how to fight it!

The Enemy's most secret and greatest weapons are our deepest fears. The Enemy uses fear and worry to prevent us from taking action and, even worse, causes us to give up. Now let's take a few moments to finish our discussion on fear and learn how to minimize its power within our lives.

The Birthplace of Fear

"Fear kills more dreams than failure ever will."
—Suzy Kassem

Society, parents, churches, and other major influences are where our fears began, at a very early age.

Think about it. What did we want to be when we grew up? Ballerinas, artists, rappers, firefighters, astronauts—the sky was the limit. Unfortunately, when we were somewhere between the ages of 13 and 18, society told us we needed to be bankers, lawyers, doctors, accountants, software engineers, and insurance reps in order to be successful. A recent study published by the Oxford Academic reveals only 6% of adults end up in careers they dreamt about as children.[7]

All of my good friends currently work or have worked in the aforementioned "successful" fields. Not one of them has ever told me this was their dream job growing up. I am 100% guilty as charged! I was a certified public accountant and financial consultant for almost 20 years because it was what I was "supposed to do."

I get it. It's scary to be different, chase our dreams, and truly be ourselves. It's even more frightening when we think about not making enough money and even worse, the fear of losing status among our

---

7   Javier G. Polavieja, Lucinda Platt, Nurse or Mechanic? The Role of Parental Socialization and Children's Personality in the Formation of Sex-Typed Occupational Aspirations, *Social Forces*, Volume 93, Issue 1, September 2014, Pages 31–61, https://doi.org/10.1093/sf/sou051.

peers. Remember, we all want to be seen, heard, loved, and relevant. So much so, we worry: the most useless form of fear ever!

What, Me, Worry?

Let's talk about the elephant in the room: worry. Ugh! What a no-good $%&*@#^&#.

Worry is one of the worst types of fear and a complete waste of our time. Worry drains us and everyone around us of our positive energy. The worry epidemic leads to desperation, bad decisions, and exhaustion. Worry opens the door wide for the Enemy to step in and wreak havoc with our lives.

Even worse, WebMD shared a study revealing how worrying can even shorten our lives.[8] The crazy part is most worries are not even real and will never come to fruition. Almost 99% of our worries are complete garbage and will never, ever come true. Wow!

But worrying about our death, politics, what Sam next door thinks, or another country invading us doesn't help anyone, especially ourselves. As we previously discussed, this is why it is so critical for us to minimize the noise all around us.

We'll know when it's time to truly be afraid—trust me, we're wired for it. If someone arrives with bad intentions, we'll handle it—and if you follow the suggestions in this book, you'll quickly spot bad intentions and remove them from your life even faster.

Worrying is about control, and we have no control—none!—outside of our mindset and choices. My goal is for all of us to live our lives filled with gratitude and abundance—not regret spending our precious time worrying and not taking action.

---

8   Goodman, Brenda. "Even Mild Anxiety May Shorten a Person's Life." WebMD. WebMD, July 31, 2012. https://www.webmd.com/mental-health/news/20120731/mild-anxiety-may-shorten-persons-life#1.

As with everything in this book, this takes practice. There's no magic pill or mystical light switch to turn off our worry. I get it. I still face worry even after many years of hardcore emotional and mental work.

Shifting from Worry to Mindfulness

Worrying is thinking about the future—and wishing for the problem to come true.

My life coach and an all-around epic human, Nancie Vito, reached the point of burnout in her career after years of focusing on depression and suicide prevention. As a result, Nancie changed careers in 2009 to become, in my humble opinion, a Legendary life coach. She now helps people flourish and get unstuck in their lives and careers. Nancie confesses to a history of chronically worrying and came to realize it was creating stress and overwhelming her. For people to get from where they are, to where they want to be, she says they need to stop worrying and start focusing on their inner game (i.e., the tough mental and emotional work discussed throughout this book).

Here are simple steps Nancie recommends to understand *why* we're worrying:

- First, become aware of the fear. (We must not give worry too much of our energy because feeding into the doubt, breeds more doubt, and can become all-consuming.)
- Ask yourself what you're really worried about.
- Consider if that fear is a real threat to you or not.

To *minimize* the worrying, Nancie walks us through these steps:
- Every thought is a choice. We may not have control over the thoughts that come in, but we can then choose what to do with them. What are you choosing to do with your thoughts?
- Notice that you are safe, right here and right now.

- Take five slow, deep breaths and say, "I am okay and safe in this moment right now."

Nancie believes another great tool to minimize worry is the practice of mindfulness. Mindfulness is defined as the quality or state of being conscious or aware of something, especially our mental and emotional state. For me, one of the easiest ways to become mindful is via the practices of gratitude and meditation. I absolutely love that Nancie, a depression expert and mental health specialist, also believes one of the best ways to minimize fear is mindfulness. Yes—As do I!

P.S. Thank you, Nancie, for being you and helping me find myself!

Conquering Fear

Worry and fear are our biggest obstacles when it comes to never giving up. In Chapter 1, we discussed how taking action is a cure for fear.

I've also learned that I can feel the fear and move forward anyway by no longer making my life and work about me.

Everything I do now is to serve others. For example, when I'm nervous about a big speaking gig, I remind myself how the speech is not about my fame, ego, or vanity. The speech is to inspire and serve the audience. If we save or serve even one life, we've won. And if my book and coaching impact one person positively, I'm winning.

Let's Finish This Thing

I recently read the book *Finish* by Jon Acuff. It was so timely as I was in the bottom of the 9th inning of finishing this book. Trust me when I tell you, writing this book has been a fistfight to the death with me, fighting my worst enemy—*myself!*

One of the hardest things to do for a lot of us is to simply start. However, a lot of people, including yours truly, have started many things, time and time again, but never finish. When we make mistakes, miss deadlines, or have setbacks, our perfectionism allows us to think it's okay to quit. As we discussed earlier, perfectionism is a killer of all things goodness, creativity, and especially finishing our work!

Even worse, in certain circumstances, we don't just quit; we spiral in the opposite direction—back into bad habits. For example, if we are trying to lose weight and slip up one day, we think, *Screw it, I'll just eat three more slices of cake and let me add a double cheeseburger for dessert.*

We do this because deep down, we believe we *failed* since we're not *perfect.* Instead, we can pick right back up where we left off, whether we are committed to eating healthy, finishing a project, or repairing a relationship. The work doesn't care if we ate a slice of cake, missed a deadline, or sent a snarly text. The work is still waiting for us.

To me, finishing what we've started is more important than simply getting started. In *Finish*, I found an epic tip shared by Jon to help us "finish the drill." He suggests either to *cut our goals in half* or *double the length of time* needed to complete them. If we want to lose ten pounds in two months, we can change the goal to five pounds or four months. Genius!

I am already seeing benefits from implementing this tactic for completing my goals. Becoming a pro means finishing the actions we start. Done is so much better than perfect.

Will We Ever Truly Finish?

I hope not! Now that we have the tools outlined throughout these chapters, I know we will finish tasks and complete goals. I know that we will be finished with energy vampires; the words *try* and *busy,* bad habits, and self-contempt. I also know we will never give up, especially if we've made it this far into the book!

However, I hope we never truly finish with the game of life or the relentless pursuit of serving others until our very last breath. I believe to the depths of my soul each of us has a purpose until the day we die. It is our job to find it, which creates a feeling of validation and fulfillment even in our later stages of life.

For me, I have no desire to retire and spend my remaining days sitting on a beach or on a golf course. What I desire is to take a three-month vacation every year as I continue to work in my zone of brilliance. I want to always be a part of and serve a greater community.

I see so many people do nothing of service or purpose when they retire, causing them to stagnate. However, nature doesn't do inertia. In the natural world, which includes us, we're either growing or dying. This is true for our mindsets, emotions, and physical bodies as well.

We must keep moving—especially our minds, hearts, brains, and bodies. If we commit to this, I know we'll find peace of mind, a sense of significance, and will leave a lasting legacy when it's time for us to leave this beautiful planet.

Burn the Boats

There's an old parable about a great general. When he and his army arrive on foreign soil for the great battle, the general decides to burn all of their boats. He tells his men: "There's only one way to go home now. It's either victory or death."

To me, this story says, "Don't let the fear of failure stop you." Chasing our dreams is hard when we're afraid of failure or judgment from others. In this parable, the army had to win, or die.

This story is a great metaphor for our lives and how seriously we need to take our dreams in order to make them happen. Why *don't* we burn our boats and chase our deepest desires? Why are we so afraid of putting it all on the line and never looking back—without letting the opinions of others, being told to be realistic, or our responsibilities stop us?

"How has being realistic or responsible kept you from
living the life you want to live?"
—Tim Ferriss

Remember, everything in life is a choice. It is up to *us* to prioritize our lives, or someone else will do it for us! We can choose to chase our dreams in baby steps by reverse engineering or taking massive action and *burning the boats*. Start investing in your knowledge to become great in whatever it is your heart desires. If I can do it, so can you!

What's the worst thing that can happen? We fail, we're laughed at, or even worse, we die? Here's the flip side of that coin: We learn from our failings and be even better the next time we chase our dream! Let them laugh—we are in the arena and the haters, naysayers, and judgers are living the lives others want them to live. We are living our lives on *our* terms fighting for our happiness in our arena! And if we die, we die doing something we love and are passionate about. Nothing can be better than that!

There's a reason so many cultures embrace their elders and seek their wisdom, guidance, and compassion. They've lived a life, seen the failures and triumphs, loved and lost, and have the scars to prove it. They'll tell us to go chase our dreams. They'll tell us to burn the boats. They will tell us to die with no regrets.

No Regrets

"Our lives get shorter by 24 hours every day!"

The last thing we want is to arrive at the end of our lives and look back with regrets. Regrets like not chasing our passions or realizing we didn't spend as much time with our friends nor travel as much as we wanted. Our time and how we spend it is all a choice. Bronnie Ware wrote a great book called *The Five Regrets of the Dying*. The following are the most common responses of those in their final days she interviewed.

I wish I had:

1. the courage to live a life true to myself, not the life others expected of me.
2. not worked so hard.
3. the courage to express my feelings.
4. stayed in touch with my friends.
5. let myself be happier.

One of my top core values is to leave this life without regrets. Because of this, I *burned the boats* when I walked away from a prestigious career and large salary that would have set me up for life. I simply couldn't work in a career because of the importance others placed upon it. I could no longer do work that neither inspired me nor made me happy. I decided to be me!

I now work in a fulfilling career coaching others to become the people they dream of being. I embrace my mistakes and failures and know they've made me the man I am today. I choose to see the gratitude and goodness in the world and work at cutting out the noise and negative influences from my life. I now prioritize travel and time spent with close friends. I embrace, "If it's not a Hell Yes, it's a No!"

I 100% believe you can and *will* have it all in your precious life. Passion, happiness, success, and peace of mind are just a few choices away. You might not be ready to burn the boats now, but with continued practice on the simple tactics outlined in this book, you will be ready sooner than you think. When the time is right and you're ready to lean in and step up to the life you were born to live, you will make a massive positive impact on yourself, your family, friends, and the communities you serve. You will become . . . and be remembered as . . . LEGENDARY!

Know this for sure, my fellow beautiful humans—I'll be standing right next to you every step of this Legendary journey. I love you all!

LEGENDARY ACTIONS & REMINDERS

- Remember: Continued action and never giving up, especially through the hardships, failures, and mistakes is where Legends are truly born.
- When overwhelmed with worry, follow Nancie Vito's simple steps to minimize the fear and to move forward in mindfulness.
- To finish a task or goal, cut the goal in half or double the length of time needed to complete them.
- If you do nothing else in this arena, keep taking action, never give up, and finish *no matter what!*

Conclusion

Let me leave you beautiful humans with this.

Recently, I heard something that floored me and made me pause and reflect: The definition of Hell is on the day we die, the person we are meets the person we could have become. Wow—talk about an epic reason for not leaving this Earth with *should haves* or *regrets*.

For almost 37 years, I did not know *life* was so precious, incredibly short, and a gift. Actually, I now believe we are granted three gifts:

1. The gift of life
2. The gift of choice
3. And the gift of death

The second gift, *choice*, is the only true power we have and the only thing in life we actually control. Absolutely nothing else is in our power or control, my dear friends.

And for the final gift, *death*, it's not *if* we'll die, it's *when*. We can be scared of death or use it as a motivator and gift, knowing our time is limited. So, *Carpe Diem*—let's seize every day to the best of our abilities!

For me, this is what I've learned and discovered to be the meaning of life:

- Give love.
- Receive love.
- Discover our purpose.
- Use our purpose to be of service to others.
- Grow and learn every day until our very last breath.

For this is what we get to do, my fellow Legends in the making. We get to put one foot in front of the other, and then repeat. We get to continue moving forward and never give up. We get to lift our eyes up and see this beautiful world once more and choose to see the goodness and beauty all around us.

We get to choose the way we think. We get to choose the way we act. We get to choose the way we feel.

For so long as fate will allow us, we get to live on for one more day! We get to *live*, my beautiful humans. We get to *live*.

I love you all!

This is me giving you a big, heartfelt, loving Tommy hug!

P.S. Now that you've finished reading the book (congratulations and thank you, by the way), please visit TommyBreedlove.com/Legendary to take a quick assessment and find out which Legendary action or reminder you need to focus on first.

Recommended Book List

This is a list of the books I've recommended or referenced throughout this book. For good measure, I've included some others on the Breedlove must read list. Not only have I read all of these wonderful and inspiring manuscripts, but I've read many of them two, three, and even four times. These books have and still make my life better, and if you take anything away from this book, let it be this, read more. The more I read, the more I realize how much I don't know!

These are in alphabetical order by author's last name and in no particular order of importance, but are all epic books.

Breedlove, Heather. *Shine Your Bright*. Atlanta, GA: BookLogix, 2018.

Brown, C. Brené. *The Gifts of Imperfection: Let Go of Who You Think You're Supposed to Be and Embrace Who You Are*. Center City, Minn.: Hazelden, 2010.

Brown Brené. *Braving the Wilderness: the Quest for True Belonging and the Courage to Stand Alone*. New York: Random House, 2019.

Brunson, Russell, and Robert T. Kiyosaki. *Expert Secrets: the Underground Playbook to Find Your Message, Build a Tribe, and Change the World*. New York: Morgan James Publishing, 2017.

Buechley, Seth. *Ambition: Leading with Gratitude*. High Bridge Books, 2018.

Carnegie, Dale, Dorothy Carnegie, and Arthur R. Pell. *How to Win Friends & Influence People*. Philadelphia: Running Press, 2017.

Chernow, Ron. *Titan: the Life of John D. Rockefeller, Sr.* New York: Vintage Books, 2004.

Chernow, Ron. *Alexander Hamilton.* London: Head of Zeus, 2017.

Clear, James. *Atomic Habits: An Easy & Proven Way to Build Good Habits & Break Bad Ones.* New York: Avery, an imprint of Penguin Random House, 2018.

Covey, Stephen. *The 7 Habits of Highly Effective People.* London: Simon & Schuster, 1999.

Coyle, Daniel. *The Talent Code: Greatness Isn't Born. Its Grown.* London: Arrow, 2010.

Cron, Ian Morgan. *The Road Back to You: an Enneagram Journey to Self-Discovery.* Seoul: Duranno, 2017.

Eker, T. Harv. *Secrets of the Millionaire Mind: Mastering the Inner Game of Wealth.* HarperCollins, 2005.

Frankl, Viktor E. *Man's Search for Meaning.* Boston: Beacon Press, 2006.

Grace, Annie, DeAndre Purdie, and Mary Purdie. *This Naked Mind: Control Alcohol: Find Freedom, Discover Happiness, & Change Your Life.* ASPN Publications, 2015.

Hardy, Darren. *The Compound Effect: Multiplying Your Success--One Simple Step at a Time.* Boston, MA: Da Capo Press, 2013.

Hendricks, Gay. *The Big Leap: Conquer Your Hidden Fear and Take Life to the Next Level.* New York: HarperOne, 2010.

Hill, Napoleon. *Think and Grow Rich!: the Original 1937 Edition.* Charleston, SC: Palmera Publishing, 2010.

Hill, Napoleon, Sharon L. Lechter, Mark Victor Hansen, and Michael Bernard Beckwith. *Outwitting the Devil: the Secret to Freedom and Success.* New York: Sterling, 2018.

Howes, Lewis. *The Mask of Masculinity: How Men Can Embrace Vulnerability, Create Strong Relationships, and Live Their Fullest Lives.* New York: Rodale, 2017.

Jeffers, Susan. *Feel the Fear and Do It Anyway*. London: Vermilion, 2012.

Kabat-Zinn, Jon. *Wherever You Go, There You Are: Mindfulness Meditation in Everyday Life*. New York: Hachette Books, 2014.

Keller, Gary, 1957- and Jay. Papasan, *The One Thing: The Surprisingly Simple Truth Behind Extraordinary Results*. Austin, Tex.: Bard Press, 2012.

Kiyosaki, Robert T., and Sharon L. Lechter. *Rich Dad, Poor Dad: What the Rich Teach*. New York: Warner Business Books, 2000.

Lakhiani, Vishen. *The Code of the Extraordinary Mind: Ten Unconventional Laws to Redefine Your Life & Succeed on Your Own Terms*. New York: Rodale, 2016.

Lamott, Anne. *Bird by Bird*. New York: Anchor Books, 1997.

Michalowicz, Mike. *Profit First: Transform Your Business from a Cash-Eating Monster to a Money-Making Machine*. New York, USA: Portfolio, 2017.

Moran, Brian, and Michael Lennington. *The 12 Week Year*. New Jersey: John Wiley & Sons, 2013.

Pavlidis, Nick. *Confessions of a Terrible Husband: Lessons Learned from a Lumpy Couch*. Boston, MA: Free Agent Press, 2015.

Peterson, Jordan B., Ethan Van Sciver, and Norman Doidge. *12 Rules for Life: an Antidote to Chaos*. Toronto: Vintage Canada, 2020.

Ramsey, Dave. *The Total Money Makeover: a Proven Plan for Financial Fitness*. Nashville, TN: Nelson Books, an imprint of Thomas Nelson, 2013.

Robbins, Anthony, and Peter Mallouk. *Unshakeable: Your Financial Freedom Playbook*. New York, NY: Simon & Schuster, 2018.

Roberts, Gregory David. *Shantaram*. London: Abacus, 2008.

Singer, Michael A. *The Untethered Soul: the Journey beyond Yourself*. Oakland, CA: Noetic Books, Institute of Noetic Sciences, New Harbinger Publications, Inc., 2013.

Tan, Chade-Meng. *Search inside Yourself: the Secret to Unbreakable Concentration, Complete Relaxation, Total Self-Control*. London: Collins, 2013.

Tolle, Eckhart. *A New Earth: Awakening to Your Life's Purpose*. London: Penguin Books, 2018.

Tolle, Eckhart. *The Power of Now: a Guide to Spiritual Enlightenment*. Sydney, NSW: Hachette Australia, 2018.

Tuff, Chris. *The Millennial Whisperer: The Practical, Profit-Focused Playbook for Working With and Motivating the World's Largest Generation*. New York: Morgan James Publishing, 2019.

Victore, James. *Feck Perfuction: Dangerous Ideas on the Business of Life*. San Francisco: Chronicle Books, 2019.

Zukav, Gary, Oprah Winfrey, and Maya Angelou. *The Seat of the Soul*. New York: Simon and Schuster, 1989.

My Daily Reading Recommendations

As part of my morning routine, I read and meditate on a passage from each of the below books each and every day.

The Holy Bible: Modern English Version. Lake Mary, FL: Passio, 2015.

Allen, James. *As a Man Thinketh: the Complete Original Edition*. New York: St. Martins Essentials, 2019.

Deng, Ming-Dao. *365 Tao: Daily Meditations*. San Francisco, CA: HarperSanFrancisco, 2006.

Fox, Matthew. *Christian Mystics: 365 Readings and Meditations*. Novato, CA: New World Library, 2011.

Holiday, Ryan. *Daily Stoic: 366 Meditations on Self-Mastery, Perseverance and Wisdom: Featuring New Translations of Seneca, Marcus Aurelius and Epictetus*. Penguin Publishing Group, 2016.

The Mother. *The Sunlit Path*. Lotus Press, 1984.

Other Daily Reading Book Recommendations

Also, in addition to my morning readings, I sprinkle a passage from the below great texts into my daily routine every day to mix it up throughout each month.

Castaneda, Carlos. *The Wheel of Time: the Shamans of Ancient Mexico, Their Thoughts about Life, Death and the Universe*. New York.: Washington Square Press, 2001.

Gibran, Kahlil. *The Prophet*. New York: Alfred A. Knopf, 2008.

Gray, Albert E. N. *The Common Denominator of Success*. Cronulla, N.S.W.: Classicbooks, 2005.

Mandino, Og. *The Greatest Salesman in the World*. New York : F. Fell, 1968.

Osteen, Joel. *I Declare: 31 Promises to Speak Over Your Life*. New York: Hachette Nashville, 2012.

Tzu, Lao. *The Tao Te Ching*. CreateSpace Independent Publishing Platform, 2018.

Tzu, Shun. *The Art of War*. CreateSpace Independent Publishing Platform, 2014.

Whyte, David. *River Flow: New & Selected Poems*. Langley, WA: Many Rivers Press, 2012.

Wuling, Shi. *The Path to Peace*. Amitabha Publications, 2006.

Acknowledgements

I am extremely humbled by and grateful for everyone who made this book actually come to fruition. It has literally been three years of blood, sweat, and tears. Each of the following people has been a special and critical part in helping me in life, success, and with completing this book.

At the top of the list is Heather Breedlove. There are no words to capture how I feel about you and what your daily support means to me. Thank you for falling in love with me the moment you saw me. I am also grateful for you always "protecting and defending this fort" and for always "showing up." You are the number one reason my life has significance.

A very special thank you goes to Lindsey Makitalo. You have been with us since day one of writing this book and have been a motivator, believer, and inspiration during every page of the writing. Your incredible attitude and willingness to do anything to make this a success has been simply awe-inspiring. Your hard work, dedication to *Legendary*, and belief in our movement are humbling and I am eternally grateful for who you are as a person and all you do. Heather and I truly do love you!

To my mom and dad, Marian and Tom Breedlove – Without you, this book would not have been possible. Thank you for pushing me in the right direction and inspiring me to make positive changes in my life. I love you.

To H.T. Ball and Marie Breedlove (aka Grammy and Pops) – You both showed me unconditional love and what family actually means through all of the pain. I miss and love you both so very much!

To Mike Hegwood – Thank you for showing me what a real man and fatherly love actually are. You were a true guiding light and inspiration for me when I was in darkness. I miss you dearly, and I love you.

To Brenda Hegwood – Thank you for being the definition of grace and class and for raising two epic children who have touched my life in unexplainable ways. You were dealt an awful and undeserved blow in life and your dignity, love, and kindness during and since are an inspiration for all of us. I love you!

To Justin Hegwood – You are the closest thing to a brother I have. Thank you for sticking with me through the ups and downs and for always calling me "family." Your love and support mean the world to me and Heather. I love you!

To Cade Joiner – My brother from another mother. You are one of my oldest friends; thank you for always being there for me through thick and thin. You are the true definition of a great man and I would literally do anything for you. Here's to 40 more years of you and me doing our best to leave this world better than we found it. I love you dearly, my brother!

To Ryan Hopkins – You are my oldest friend and you were there on the night my entire life changed. Thank you for always being there, never judging, and for loving me unconditionally. I would literally do anything for you. Thank you for years of friendship and brotherhood. I love you dearly, my brother.

To Chris Tuff – You are the closest thing to a best friend I've ever had. Your affirmations, love, and never wavering belief in me, my work, or this project will never be forgotten. Anytime…. anywhere…. my brother – I will always be there for you!

To Nick Pavlidis – Your patience, flexibility, coaching, and guidance have been invaluable for the three long years of this project. You are truly a man of great character and service. Thank you for being the brains and quarterback behind this book.

To Sarah Tuff Dunn – Thank you for literally saving us and for your talent and brilliance in all things writing and editing. This book would simply have never been finished without your hard work, dedication, and belief in the project. Your kindness and support will never be forgotten.

To Julie Tuff – Thank you for your kindness, love, and support with helping me be a more healthy person, man, and husband. Our deep chats mean the world to me and you are quite possibly the best and most kind mom I have ever met. I look forward to calling you a dear friend until my very last breath.

To Michael Liss – You are by far the most interesting and kind person I have ever met. Thank you for always believing in me and everything I do. I miss you. Come home soon, my brother!

To Kerry Geho – Thank you for being one of the great male figures and mentors in my life. You always keep me grounded, love me unconditionally, and are there for me when I need it most. Because of you, I am now living my life and not my story.

To Clay Stapleford – Thank you for always seeing the best in me and reminding me that a positive mindset and belief in myself are essential to happiness and success. You are one of my true brothers in life and our early morning coffees and late-night talks are some of my favorite moments. I love you, my brother, and am proud to call you a friend!

To Lori Geisler – My sister in life and my friend. Thank you for always allowing me to be vulnerable and honest without ever judging. I look forward to so many more worldwide adventures and our epic conversations for many years to come. I love you and am proud to call you my friend!

To the Great Eight! – (Chris Tuff, Hank McLarty, Quincy Jones, Marc Hodulich, Bert Weiss, Taylor Barnes and Dr. Peter Boulden) – You are my brothers in arms and the majority of my inner circle. This group literally is changing the world and will continue to make a great impact on each other. Quincy Jones, thank you for the foresight and wisdom to put such a fine group of men together. Bert Weiss, for always being vulnerable and calling people out. Taylor Barnes, for modeling what a man of God, a servant father, and a loving husband truly is. To Hank McLarty, for your dedication to being the best man and father you can be and for always getting up after being knocked down. To Mark Hodulich, for always doing hard things and for helping others go beyond their limits to accomplish their dreams. To Pete, for modeling what humble success looks like by building an empire from scratch with your own two hands. To Chris Tuff, see above, my brother! You all make me better in life and business and as a husband to Heather. I truly love and respect you all so dearly!

To Darrah Brustein – For being one of the first to inspire me to go out and chase my dreams of making this world a better place. You have always been a great friend, confidant, and shoulder to lean on in my times of need. I hope I have been the same for you. You are a great friend and I love you. I look forward to many more adventures together.

To Kevin and Megan Ouzts – Your friendship, love and laughter mean more to Heather and me than you possibly know. Thank you for showing me that working hard, chasing your dreams and just caring a little more are goals worth fighting for. Here's to many more years of goodness together!

To Lane Beene – Mr. Top Gun himself. You are a beacon of class and a true man of integrity. Thank you for being a brother and an accountability partner for me and for always helping me to be a better man. I am honored and proud to call you my friend.

To Aaron Walker – For being a great coach, mentor, and inspiration in my life as well as the lives of so many other men. You are certainly one of the closest people I know who has actually earned the title of Legendary. Thank you for never compromising your beliefs or values and allowing men like me to aspire to live a life of significance and leaving a lasting legacy in this world.

To Tom Schwab – You were the initial inspiration for this book when you heard my story. I would have never thought of writing a book much less telling my story to the world. Thank you for being a positive force and inspiration in my life and for helping so many people find their voice in this world. I am proud to call you my friend and my door is always open to you.

To Dan Miller – Thank you for all of the inspiring conversations about all things love, serving, and helping ourselves and others be better humans. You are true brightness in a world that can seem so dark at times. I cannot wait to see what the future holds for our friendship.

To Nancie Vito – For helping me find my purpose in life and the courage to leave the corporate world behind. Your inspiring guidance as a life coach has improved not only my life, but the lives of thousands of men because of our work together. Know you are planting the seeds for so much goodness to come into this world.

To Alvaro Arauz – For being a great inspiration and cheerleader for me along my journey of chasing this dream. You are one of the great humans in my life and it has been my honor to have you as a trusted confidant and good friend. Here's to many more Hawks games together, my brother.

To Mike Wien – For being my first business coach and mentor. Your guidance and wisdom have been invaluable to me. You are a true networking and marketing genius and an all-around great human. Thank you for helping me find my specific edge in this world.

To Gyl Grinberg – For being a trusted resource, friend, and great source of wisdom in guiding me through life's big decisions. I look forward to watching our friendship continue to grow and flourish for many years to come, my brother.

To Kedar Brown – A true sage and spiritual leader in my life. I really don't know why I was called to follow you into those North Carolina mountains, but I did and will never forget it. You have touched and healed so many lives, including mine.

To all of my clients – Thank you for showing up each and every day to be better than you were yesterday. It is truly my honor to walk this journey with you and to watch as you build and live Legendary Lives. You all help me to be a better leader, man, and husband!

To John Stapleton – Thank you for the amazing cover designs. You are a very talented and great man. Thank you for sharing your brilliance with this project.

A special thank you goes out to the research, writing, and editing team with Authority Ghostwriting led by the great Nick Pavlidis. And specifically to my man Mr. Ethan Webb – Your reviews and research were invaluable and thank you for believing in the work.

To Jennifer Harshman and your entire editing team – You all are an extremely talented group and thank you for the love and kindness you showed our message and our work.

To Onsite Workshops – For allowing me to *feel* for the very first time in 36 years and for starting me on this journey of building and living a Legendary Life. Your work and helping me break free will never be forgotten.

I also want to thank Delta Airlines as I've written the majority of this book sitting on their planes. Their excellent service has been a major factor in getting this book completed. Also, my dad was a Delta mechanic for many years, so it's great to keep the loyalty within the family.

And last but certainly not least, thank you to my publisher, Morgan James, led by the incredible David Hancock. I am very grateful for your team, support, flexibility, and patience with watching *Legendary* come to life. Thank you for taking the risk and you made this book powerful and special!

Neither I nor this book would be here without all of the amazing humans above. I am eternally grateful and humbled, and I love you all. Thank you.

About the Author

Tommy Breedlove is an Atlanta-based business, relationship, and mindset coach who is a regular featured keynote speaker at global events.

Tommy started his 20-year corporate career at one of the largest financial consulting firms in the world, and eventually became a shareholder, the International Practice Leader, and a member of the board of directors for one of the largest public accounting and financial firms in the southeast U.S.

Photo credit: Michelle Rose

At the top of his career, Tommy experienced a transformational moment inspiring him to walk away from the corporate world to change his life and follow his true calling.

Tommy now serves clients and audiences everywhere by empowering them to build and live Legendary Lives. He guides people to discover a life of significance while building a lasting legacy. The simple tools he shares shows them how to work in their zone of brilliance, obtain financial freedom, and live with meaning and balance. The goal is to help everybody to become the person they've always wanted to be.

When Tommy isn't speaking or serving his clients, he enjoys traveling the world, hiking, and spending quality time with his wife and two dogs.

Join the conversation and follow Tommy on Instagram @ tommybreedlove.

9 781642 795530